Amazing Gracie

David Earle Steward

Copyright: 2008 David E. Steward. All rights preserved

No part of this book may be reproduced, stored in a retrieved system,
or transmitted by any means without the written permission of the author.

First Published by David E. Steward 5/2/08

ISBN: 978-0-6152-0677-6

Printed by: Lulu.com

Printed in the United States of America

My sincere thanks to all… in Palm Springs, Palm Desert and The Coachella Valley, and in the cities of Beverly Hills, West Hollywood, Los Angeles and Orange County, and elsewhere, whose images and names appear in this book…when asked permission to include them, all gave similar responses…*"Please do"*… *"It will be an honor"*… *"Oh, of course "*… *"You didn't even have to ask"*… *"For our little Gracie, it will certainly be our pleasure"*.   Again…I thank you all.

David E. Steward … *"Gracie's Dad"*

A portion of the proceeds from the sale of this book will be distributed to selected Organizations and Causes, which fight for the rights and welfare of animals, and those that fight against any unjust acts against animals …wherever they may be.

"Man's best friend"… an awesome title to bestow upon anyone. However, since very early times, the domesticated dog (canis) has worn it most deservedly. Evidence suggests that "man" didn't domesticate them; women did it. Be that as it may, all of us who have had the joyous experience of one or more of them in our lives, can certainly understand why…"we all feel ours is special… and rightly so". Their bravery, intelligence and unconditional love would surely be enough, but for anyone not to also recognize that each has a distinct and unique personality…with feelings of happiness, compassion, jealousy, sadness or grief … has never watched with an eye of true comprehension. In his book "The Pawprints of History", psychologist and renowned dog-expert Stanley Coren writes, "paw prints… along with man's footprints…have been recognized and recorded in the sands of history. These four-footed witnesses, large and small, have been catalysts, close companions and a defining influence on some of our great and historical men and women… Florence Nightingale, Dr. Sigmund Freud, King Charles II, Fifth Dalai Lama, George Washington, Calvin Coolidge and Bill Clinton…all who consequently performed distinctive deeds that influenced the course of world events".

Over the centuries, the bloodlines of most breeds have changed little. As a result the Poodle of today…with its "something more human than canine" quality… has remained a magnificent, sophisticated, and most intelligent breed. Their sometimes weird and wonderful grooming comes from the ancient practice of leaving generous amounts of hair around their joints and chest areas to protect them from the chilling water they were compelled to jump into, as they retrieved their master's wounded feathered spoils. Today, this grooming is for show purposes only, and hardly defines the great heart and courage of this fine animal. Now the desire to achieve a smaller version of this special animal: from the magnificent Royal Standard Poodle, to the smaller Miniature, and then the Toy, comes the smallest…the Teacup. For what its worth, the American Kennel Association has yet to recognize it as a "pure breed" and is disqualified for show. Nevertheless…the Teacup Poodle produces "unadulterated pleasure" for its owner and for all who observe it…and although smaller in stature… still maintains the bloodlines of integrity and intelligence of the breed.

This is the story of Gracie…my own *"True Champion"*… and the *paw prints* she left forever on my heart…and on the hearts of so many others.

David E. Steward

Some Favorite Quotes

"No matter how little money and how few possessions you own, having a dog makes you rich" -- Louis Sabin

"I care not for a man's religion, whose dog and cat are not the better for it"

-- Abraham Lincoln

"The greatness of a Nation and its moral progress, can be judged by the way its animals are treated" -- Mahatma Gandhi

"If you have men who will exclude any of God's creatures from the shelter of compassion and pity, you will have men who will deal likewise with their fellow men"

-- St. Francis of Assisi

" If you think you are a person of some influence, try ordering someone's dog around"

-- Cowboy Wisdom

"A dog is not almost human, and I know of no greater insult to the canine race than to describe it as such" -- John Holmes

"To err is human, to forgive, canine" -- Unknown

" All animals are equal, but some are more equal than others" -- George Orwell – Author

" Man is the only animal that blushes – or needs to" -- Mark Twain

" Histories are more full of examples of the fidelity of dogs than of friends" –

-- Alexander Pope

"Some of my best leading men, have been dogs and horses" -- Elizabeth Taylor

" There are two kinds of people, those who love animals and those I don't care to meet"

-- Rudyard Kipling

"The little furry buggers are just deep, deep wells you throw all your emotions into" --

-- Bruce Schimmel"

"Until one has loved an animal, a part of one's soul remains unawakened"

-- Anatole France

" A dog wags its tail… with its heart" --Martin Buxbaum

"An animals eyes have the power to speak a great language" -Martin Buber

"Life is as dear to a mute creature as it is to man. Just as one wants happiness and fears pain, just as one wants to live and not die, so do other creatures" --

His Holiness The Dalai Lama

Gracie...was an experience...mystical, magical, and unforgettable. To fully express her loving effect on me, and on so many others... even with all the words written here, and with all the memories vividly recalled...best said, *I, who was considered a teacher of love, again became a pupil...and therefore learned even more...how to love... and to be loved.*

Perhaps my fondest wish ... is that you will too.

David

Gracie

"The little dog that everybody loved…"

Grace' Of Countryside Deva

When full-grown...Grace' (ie) was 5 ½ pounds of Teacup Poodle. She had one 4½-pound sister, named Peaches. Throughout the years, Gracie became more like a "Tea-Pot" (6--7 lbs.). Perhaps at times a little overweight, but her "marvelous silver markings, under a phantom blue topcoat", with a preferred, always perfectly maintained ... "Special-for-Gracie, Teddy Bear groom"... and along with her unusually arresting eyes and face... could send admirers into sometimes unintelligible, but always endearing, baby talk. Gracie was agreeably "one of the cutest, most loveable, and irresistible creatures ever." Moreover, her notable intelligence, deep loyalty, and a charming dichotomy of sweet sophistication, impulsive mischief, and engaging personality...made her truly...."One of a kind".

Of course, that's just part of the story...so, "told in her own words" ...*Heeere's Gracie...*

Hello, my name is Gracie... and that's my "Dad". I have had a good life. He says "An Amazing one" and that I should tell it... So with a little help from him ... *here and there* ...

I don't know if Dad wanted me to go back this far, but here are some things that happened before we met. I was born in Perris California. (Dad would later tell jokingly that I was "born in Paris"). One of the first things I remember...even before my eyes were open...but with my nose and appetite working very well...that I was hungry. Mom was there, with warm milk, and when I got sleepy or cold... a warm stomach, and a warm tongue, (I got bathed a lot). Early on, I noticed I was sharing my feeding times with someone else. It was my sister (Peaches). As we grew, and our eyes were open, something within us made us want to 'play and bite and growl and wrestle and sleep'.

I didn't really know who, or what I was, but somehow, deep within me, I already knew about many things…how to live, and how to survive. My father was around… sometime, but after a quick sniff or two, he pretty much left us alone. Mom acted like this was all right though, and took good care of us, especially when we needed love and encouragement. We got plenty of that, and I was happy.

Every day, a huge, tall, two-legged creature, that mom said was called a *human*, or *woman*, would come in and bring food for her. Then sometimes, pick us up very high into the air, and hold us and make funny sounds. Because it didn't hurt, we soon got used to it… somewhat. Then one day mom said…." You, and your teeth are growing fast, and it's time to start *chewing*… on something else. She really meant it, and though continuing to love us, would hardly let us "eat" again. The "tall, two-legged human" brought us food in little bowls…that we learned to eat from… and enjoy. Mom said we were in "a breeders" home and that she would explain it all later. Mom called us by "high pitched" sounds and didn't 'call us' by a name, but by our spirit. She *taught* us many things about female humans, called *woman or she,* and male humans, called *man or he,* and our living with them, and why. She said they call us *"dogs"…(that… was* a long story)…. and there are many different kinds of us, and that humans' choose us, first usually because of the way we look, and then for our personalities. And for either one, or both, we become recipients of their love, and become, a part of families, or companions of individuals. They give us *names*, and endearingly call us their "pets", or "children". She said they feed us, usually take good care of us and sometimes even spoil us, but exceptions to this were… ill-bred humans, bullies, untrained young children, or a family with other pets. She said not always…but sadly…too many. However, *she said, "Those who really love and care for us …will not let those things happen".*

Mom said we (*canines*) were born with special abilities…to heal, to predict natural occurrences, and also special senses that serve others in many ways. I didn't understand it all, but I believed her. Then she said something particularly profound concerning humans and us, and that later I would understand it… much more …*"We are an advanced civilization, more older and complete than theirs. We are gifted with extended senses, some they lost or never attained, and we listen to voices they shall never hear. We are not underlings; we are other nations, caught with them in the net of life and time, fellow prisoners of the splendor and travail of the earth"…* This was really over my head, but it felt right and that I *would* learn much more about it later, but for now… I just wanted to go play… then eat and sleep…and in that order. Then Mom said…because my sister and I were *two-colors*, we were called *"parti-poodles".* And with a little smile in her voice, she said, "You are very special", and gave us some extra kisses. Weeks passed. Every day together we all grew very close …and physically stronger.

Then one morning, something terrible happened. I woke up early from a sound overnight sleep and could not find Peaches…or Mom. I thought they might be hiding from me so I began to look everywhere. I called them. No answer. My heart sank. I had never felt loneliness or sadness before. It really hurt. Suddenly, Mom appeared…I was so happy to see her, but I could also feel that she was sad. Then she explained that during the night, humans had taken Peaches away, along with some others of our young friends, to a big city called Hollywood. There they would be on display in cages, so other humans could look at them, and if they liked them, would *pay money* to take one or two of them to live in their home. She said many humans did this and that most were good to us, but we could only hope for the best. I could not fully grasp all this… I just knew I missed Peaches and that I was sad. Mom and I cried together, and we became very close. Things became a little better. I finally had to settle into a routine without Peaches, but I could not forget her, and I wondered if I would ever see her again.

Then, for what seemed to me like a *very long time* …several days passed. One morning I heard human voices talking and laughing and then suddenly…I could not believe my eyes…there was Peaches…running toward me. We kissed and played and cried for joy. This was wonderful. She had brought two humans with her, a male and a female. They seemed nice and picked me up…firmly, but tenderly… and made loving sounds that somehow made me feel good about them. They then indicated to the 'breeding lady', that they wanted to take me home with them. She objected at first, saying "because of my unusual and defined coloring", she had planned to "keep me for breeding stock", and that "therefore I was worth much more". However, with words of persuasion…and offering more of what they called *money*… they changed her mind.

Even though mom had said this might happen to me some day, and though I was so glad to see Peaches, I felt sad having to leave her. I had rarely even been outside of the house. Suddenly we were all in *"a big cage on wheels"*, which Peaches said was called a car, and I was on my way to somewhere new. Everything was moving so fast I felt myself trembling. I was both excited and afraid. I was really missing mom. However, with encouragement from Peaches and the warm feelings I felt from the humans, I calmed down a bit. And with the soothing vibrations and rhythmic sounds of the 'big cage', plus a warm lap, and Peaches there, I finally fell asleep. I later awoke to these new surroundings, and now found myself quite calm and strangely enjoying it... It was a long trip, especially for me, but we stopped once along the way for us to play a little and for us to *"use the grass"*. Then we were on our way again. During this long trip, I asked Peaches to tell me what had happened to her the day she was taken. She said o.k…

"We were taken to a city called West Hollywood, near Los Angeles, and on Santa Monica Blvd., to a place they called a Pet Store. I was put into a cage, and on display. During the day this strange place was noisy and smothery. The loneliness was terrible, but more terrifying during the night. I cried for mom and for you. The others there cried also. Throughout my loneliness though, I remembered things Mom had said, and felt I had to be strong and face the circumstances. During the day, many humans passed by. Every kind word or gesture was welcomed as a hope of getting out of that cage and somehow returning home. I couldn't give up, but after awhile, it seemed hopeless…for as humans poked their fingers through the cage to touch me, and though many seemed to like me, apparently my price was too high. Time passed, and with naps to ease the pain and the little sleep I managed at night, helped... but my dreams of you and mom ...made the memories too vivid for me to really rest.

Then one day, between one of my early morning naps, a miracle happened! I was awakened by a strangely "familiar voice", coming from a beautiful female human. We made eye contact and I instantly felt "her aura of love"... It was like the love from mom, except this was from a human.... With gentle and loving hands she took me out of the cage and into her arms; Her "musical voice" spoke straight to my heart and all my instincts told me...*this is right.* Suddenly I wanted to belong to this human more than anything, and I knew she felt the same. The male human "felt" very kind also. My heart was beating very fast with anticipation...would they...could they take me...yes!! They paid the money for me, and my heart sang. However as we were leaving... I was sad for the others, but somehow... felt they understood... and that they were happy for me. I hoped they would all soon be rescued, and all find love and freedom. I loved my new home. They named me Peaches (my coloring). Her name was Andrea, and his name was James. She was my "*new parent, and my alpha female leader*". I felt much the same about the *alpha male.* We continued to get acquainted...and I loved the way they *'made over me'.* I was truly home.

(This is Andrea, my Mom, June, a friend
...And David, your Dad) ...**Peaches**

After the third day, and in the car, (which I had begun to like) we all visited their human friend, David, in North Hollywood. I had overheard them talking, and that she...*'my new alpha female, Andrea'*, and he, had once been... something they called *married.* He seemed special to them both. He lived in a big three-story house, built on the side of a huge hill, overlooking a valley, where you could see forever, and a place they called Universal City. The house inside seemed like some huge cave (very high vaulted ceilings), with three flights of *soft bouncy carpeted* stairs, huge rooms to play in, and large redwood balconies, on each level, with little wire fences around the bottom to keep *'us'* from falling through. It was great.

Anyway...back to him...As soon as we had entered his home they put me down to run free. Seeing me he gave a loud and endearing expression of joy. He picked me up and held me tenderly in his hands, and then very close. I felt the same love and safety from him. He was thanking them for bringing me. (It seems that earlier, they had all talked about getting pets) After a few awkward moments, they lovingly explained that "they had not brought me to live with him, but the visit was just to show me to him". His disappointment was apparent, but he quickly expressed his joy for them having me, and bringing me to see him. They were so moved by his loving reaction to me, that on the way home, I heard them plan to find out where I had originally come from, if maybe there were more, like me, and to surprise him with 'someone'. I thought of you. They made some calls, found out where, and today we made this trip to get you, for him… and here we are… heading for his house and your new home"…

…I was truly captivated by Peaches' story. And in particular, the loving behavior of these humans, which made me feel close to them too.

Soon we arrived at the man's home. I was still nervous not knowing exactly what to expect. The wide front entrance to the house was impressive, but was practically right on the street and had very little front yard, however inside… it was the way Peaches had described it…and even more. We went in and they put us both down to run free. Soon the man named David came up some stairs to greet us. Again…there were exclamations of joy and endearment. To my surprise…the man got on his hands and knees, then sat down, and then laid down flat on the floor. Impulsively, Peaches and I took advantage and smothered him with *puppy breath kisses*. He played with us both. Peaches parents also sat down. Then, still sitting on the floor, he held me…and nuzzled me… and made endearing communications with my heart. Immediately and mutually, it was… Love … and we bonded. Instinctively I knew this was right…and at that moment… *"I met…"My Dad"…the human…who would become my best friend, my alpha leader, and my unconditional love …for the rest of my life".*

When Peaches finally left, but promising to come back soon, I settled in and Dad and I began getting acquainted. At first, my crying at night was a little noisy, but soon I was 'too happy for words'. (Dad laughs). He was kind, easy to love and loved me…and that was all that mattered. One morning though…I awoke and was alone. Where was Dad? That helpless feeling of loneliness came pouring over me. I cried out loud. I missed Mom and Peaches. I was afraid. Then I heard (felt) Dad's footsteps hurrying down the stairs. He had heard me crying. He spoke, held me close, and his loving voice *spoke to my heart* and made everything all right. As I matured, I got a little better about being left alone when it was necessary, … however, because Dad sensed that…I seldom ever was.

My A.K.C. Certification papers, gotten from the breeder, said my mother's 'pedigreed' name was "Deva of Countryside" and my father's was "Countryside's Sparkling Deva". Mine was …"Grace' of Countryside Deva". Dad said he loved me even without any papers. (My name Grace'…is pronounced Gracie). Dad liked it. He said I was graceful, and that my coloring, mannerisms and attitude, lent their influence. Peaches got some papers too. (I thought of Mom…and how happy she would be for Peaches and me.)

I was smart and a fast learner; however because I was young, I had to learn some obedience routines, and build up my trust. I was taught with patience, and much love. Sometimes when I didn't listen, hitting the palm of his hand (but never hitting me) with a rolled up newspaper, usually got my attention. I remember once, to get *my undivided attention*, when I was not being too cooperative in listening to some instruction, that might one day save my life, Dad held me in a submissive position, put my whole muzzle, up to my eyes, in his mouth, and growled forcefully once or twice. It really frightened me, but it triggered something within me that I never forgot. It reminded me *that he was my alpha leader and that I could always trust in him.* Had he not, I would have instinctly taken the role, for by nature, we either lead, or are led. However, *I was always allowed and encouraged by him to have plenty of fun... And honey...we did.*

To teach me *"where"*... whenever I felt an urge to *pee-pee or poo*...for about three days he used a large training cage (in our room and always in view) with a bed (towel), and water, and a *spread newspaper*. It worked. Later, to make things easier for him, and me, and especially when it was raining or cold... outside, on one end of the bedroom balcony, dad put down a large sheet of heavy black plastic, bought several blocks of real grass from a nursery, and made me a "lawn". He cleaned it after "me"... watered it, and as it grew, even had to trim it with hedge shears. It worked well. I loved to go walking every morning, and when we did, he always carried a plastic bag or two. My poo wasn't very big, but I guess he just felt a personal obligation, to us and to others, to pick it up.

My new house was great. In it...besides always hearing (feeling) sounds (music playing), all kinds of groups, men and women singing (which I didn't pay much attention to, but he sure did)... Dad seemed to love having flowers and trees and mirrors inside. So there were flowers, several small trees all over the place and "a fountain with girl pouring water" in front of a huge mirror, and a tree on each side. The water sounds made me feel thirsty and other ways too. And when I looked into any of the mirrors they reflected a 'mystery person', but a very cute one...that looked a lot like me. Two male humans, Joseph and Eddie, also lived here. I soon relaxed around them, because they were good to me and loved to play with me. I didn't have an alpha female, but Dad often had female humans over for visits... they really 'made over me' and liked me so much they sometimes even '*stayed over*'. I really liked the females... and apparently... *so did he.*

Dad's (our) bedroom was down two sections of carpeted stairs, and with each step 'higher than me', was a challenge. At first, Dad either carried me up or down, or took it slow. After a few days, we made it a game, and soon raced up and down. At first, he let me win, but later I grew strong and held my own. We had a huge bedroom, and bed (with steps for me), big fireplace, and the large glass doors (that folded), opening onto the large redwood balcony. (And sure enough, that little wire fence to protect us from falling through). There was a huge walk-in closet, big enough to hide in, to play in, and hide my toys in. The bathroom, practically all mirrored, was very large, with a big shower and a separate Jacuzzi tub... to be bathed, and also great to play in. Upstairs was the living room and kitchen, and up more stairs, to the upper landing and front entrance, was Dad's large office. Two walls of the kitchen-breakfast-room were all glass, down to the floor; it was like standing on the edge of a cliff. It was a *breathtaking* view. The dining room was usually pretty busy, but for my health, and even though I gave "Oscar performances... with looks that could pull food out of a rock"... Dad was rarely persuaded to feed me from the table...(rarely). Others were also warned not to. Even though I wasn't that hungry...*Dad was eating!* The living room then led out onto another big wooden balcony, overlooking the treetops in our back yard and onto a huge grass covered field, also surrounded by beautiful trees. There were sounds of many birds. Sometimes we saw deer, rabbits, and an occasional coyote. Frequently at night, we heard a large pack of them chasing something. Their *'chorus of songs', with strangely familiar, wild and eerie lyrics, told me of their hunger...of the chase...and then of their 'thankfulness' for its success.* I indicated I wanted to meet them... Dad said... *he didn't think so.*

Occasionally, when explosives or gunfire were to be used for a movie, in order to be prepared for it, Universal Studios would send out leaflets, announcing to the neighborhood the days and the times. At first I was frightened, but I got used to it...*after dad picked me up and hugged me and held me in the safety of his arms...I always liked that part.*

The movie "Beethoven" was being made...about a huge, and sweet Saint Bernard. We watched the action from our balcony. There were big bright lights, colored striped tents, equipment, lots of people and several animals. We could even hear some of the speaking parts. I wanted to meet "the big boy", but Dad said "maybe someday", (but it never happened.) After the shooting ended, big noisy helicopters would sometimes land, apparently with "Celebrities, or other Big Shots" (Dad's words), because big long black cars (limousines) would be there to meet them. Farther down the field toward the studios, we could see some scenes from the movie "Jaws" being shot in a very large pool, *where a big mechanical shark... would rise up... and try to eat a boat.*

Months passed and I grew healthy and strong. Dad and I were by now, easily *reading* each other and *very impressed with each other's abilities.* My hearing, my ability to smell, and my physical dexterity were quickly multiplied. Human spirits and movements were quickly read by my senses...and by their walk, smells and sounds, I quickly learned to avoid human feet, unless they were Dad's...*He always knew where I was.* I never felt that I was "little" and I always faced life with confidence and curiosity. Big dogs, big people, big Harley's...none of these really frightened me...(However, Dad was always close by). Of course there were times when "discretion was the better part of valor" (in Dad's words) so I fittingly..."headed for the hills"...(to Dad's arms, or out of sight).

I loved our routines. On our walks, up or down the hills on Blair Street, we met lots of humans... Dad said "famous people", One was for his television part on "Fresh Prince of BelAire" and was an avid motorcycle rider. I heard Dad call him Alfonso. At times, when seeing us out front in the garage, he would stop by and talk to dad...about motorcycles, his love for racing cars...and to pet me. It seemed though...that *most* of our other neighbors...were lots of "sweet female humans". One (*special one*) named "Cricket" invited us in to have lunch, and even dinner. I liked that. We became quite friendly with others also. Dad seemed happy about all this... *Humans up here sure were nice.*

Once when we were out walking, further up the hill and around a corner or two, "A pretty lady, with blonde hair and ample breasts, (Dad's description), drove by in a big pink convertible, top down, and smiled...He said she looked familiar (famous). We continued walking and soon saw her car parked in front of a house. The house was up a hill, with lots of steps leading up to it. She was standing in the entranceway. Dad spoke...she spoke...called to me...I started up the steps... and we all got acquainted. This was her home. I thought her name *Roxanne* was pretty, and she said she liked my name too. She was sweet to me. Anyway, we visited her, and Dad always seemed "very happy" when we did. I loved to play in her house, which she seemed to enjoy me doing. In the living room, she had a very long couch, on which we sat and talked and sometimes she hugged me...and sometimes, when we were leaving...Dad too. *Happy days...for everyone.* Another of our favorite places to walk was around the big beautiful Hollywood Reservoir, close to a huge HOLLYWOOD sign.... And there were always lots of other humans and their "furry kids" walking. It was great. Some might think Dad walked me excessively, but I loved it and believe me, even though I seemed to have endless energy, if I gave any indication of fatigue, or even if he just suspicioned it, he would pick me up, or we would just stop and take a breather. I could also let him know *just by stopping.* He always carried water and a few snacks. Life was real good... here in the Hollywood Hills.

Dad found two groomers for me (Lisa and Sue), at "4 Paws Only" in the beautiful Burbank/Toluca Lake area. Sometimes we took walks in this beautiful neighborhood, where Dad said, some nice humans named Bob and Delores Hope had a home. And then just up a few blocks, and across the street from Burbank Studios, was a great Mexican Food Restaurant and Bar. There were some very friendly waitresses... so we were always welcomed in the Bar area, where we got a booth. The food was great*, or so dad said*, because...again, for my health sake, I seldom got any. Then, as the Studio was just across the street... and because we needed the exercise after *his meal*, Dad and I would walk along the sidewalk in the afternoon, where 'long lines of humans' were waiting outside...to get into the early taping of the Johnny Carson Tonight Show. Usually from them...*we got lots of attention, invitations for hugs, and 'our own standing ovations'*... *Perhaps my earliest taste of 'Show Business'.*

I had two worlds. One...just happy being at home and enjoying our morning walks... with its many different sounds, and the adventures promised to me by the many smells on every tree and bush along the way. I knew Dad felt the same way about our tranquil life together. But then... our other world... with its many places to go, and people to meet!!

I was always excited to go with him. Everywhere we went...trips to Post Offices or restaurants, or just on the streets...turned into an adventure. We became well known in many places. Some times, while talking with the people who came in and 'made over me', our visits would last a very long time. <><> At one *Post Office,* we become well acquainted with the man that *ran* the place. His name was Frank. He was Armenian. On occasion, we were invited to his home for an Armenian family dinner. *Dad said it was delicious.* Frank also owned an automobile that Dad admired...*a beautiful, vintage, cream colored, tan and brown leather appointed, Rolls Royce Silver Cloud* (Dad's words). We rode in it sometimes and it seemed to make Dad feel very good. I enjoyed it too...*just to be with him.* Dad made Music Videos, so we used it sometimes as a 'prop' for Dad's clients that he made 'promo shots' for. (I got in some of them). <><> Dad took me on visits to his dentist, whose name was Dr. Diamond. Dad said he was 'appropriately named'. He had a receptionist who was very friendly to me... *and to Dad.* She held me most of the time we were there. Later she rode in our boat. Dad said she was very pretty, (*but not prettier than me.*) I was happy. <><> A restaurant on Ventura Blvd., welcomed us. One day, we saw a lady there named Mary Hart. Dad said she was "TV famous". Not seeing us, she was paying very close attention to the person with her, so Dad didn't disturb her. We certainly could have, but Dad said, sometimes it was 'just not proper'. <><> Peaches' Mom *(who also rode a Harley)* invited us to a famous Recording Studio to watch, and hear her sing. It was fun playing there in their big recreation room. We also met some men there and Dad played pool with them. They were singers and were called "Metallica"*(Naturally, they were famous too).* That day we, and Peaches' Mom, had ridden the Harleys, and they seemed to really like *them...and her too.* We were certainly hard to miss...anywhere. <><> Even though he felt bad having to do it, Dad took me to The Holistic Animal Hospital, for an operation called "spaying". I had been... *displaying, and causing, some frisky' body language; amid some handsome and cute canine neighbors (a cute Shitzu and a very sweet pit bull)* so he knew it was time. He felt that I was too small to have "pups", even though... *they would have been beautiful and I a good mom,* he felt it was best to do it. It really didn't bother me too much, but I hated that they had to shave my cute tummy and put some ugly yellow liquid on it. I had a 'stitch' or two and felt pretty 'grown up'. (Later, we would become very involved in "*championing spaying and neutering*", to help slow down the cruel over-population of animals...especially dogs and cats.) <><> We had lots of visitors at our home and one, a close friend named Laura, was "pretty, and very sweet to me". Sometimes... *she liked me so much* ...she spent the night. Dad was very friendly to everyone that was friendly to me, and he made lots of friends that way.

Dad had many friends and so naturally I became everyone's pet. Also since Dad was the *Alpha Leader* of something called ..."church"...dozens of people came over often, to hear him talk, or just for visits. These were all called *"members",* and *"very special people"* to Dad... and to me... and to each other. Dad also tried to visit each one of them at least every week. Sometimes more, sometimes less, but... *we had a ball trying.* <><><> Besides our frequent visits to see Peaches and her 'parents'... Two other special humans that we visited often were Susan and Robin... who lived in Glendale. There Dad and I always got hugs...and good food...and who could ask for more. (We always enjoyed a visit to The Glendale Galleria...to shop, and be seen.) Another sweet female named Kathy, had a large condominium and great pool in Garden Grove, and sometimes we stayed there for 3 or 4 days, (or longer). Also Doug and Nancy were gracious, had a big house in Buena Park, and liked me, and sometimes we stayed there for a week. Also something real special to look forward to was the weekends when everyone would gather there for pool parties, volleyball, great food and fellowship. The nearby park, where we played

Volleyball, became an endless exercise regimen for me, and to keep my (and Dad's) waistline trim and proper... (Well...that was always *a work in progress*.) <><><> At our house, everyone especially seemed to enjoy the barbeques on the lower Patio... and where many gathered in and around the large hot tub under a big enclosed redwood canopy. Peaches always came over and we shared the popularity together. We loved to be pampered and grew to love many humans; however, as we Poodles are inherently "one person followers", our alpha leaders were never very far away. All the humans I had met had been friendly, lovable, and ready to play. I remembered mom said, "There were some bad ones", but so far, I had only met good ones. When it was necessary... and that was very seldom, I was only left with Peaches', or she with me. <><><> Dad also had *'toys'*: His car, two motorcycles and a sailboat. (He had earlier sold his van and airplane). I loved to ride in the car. We had a ritual. I would get in first, hop over to the passenger seat, and then, after he placed a white silk pillow in the crook of his left arm, hop back to Dad and the pillow where I always rode... and when I wasn't sleeping, had a great view.

I loved our sailboat ..."*The Family's Jewel*" (a rare, wooden hulled, 28 ft., Thunderbird) that Dad kept in a place called Marina Del Rey. It was beautiful there. The sky, the water, the boats, the people, the grass, the sand, the restaurants, the.... ok, ok... so I get carried away for a moment, but it was almost more than my small six-pounds could absorb... but I gave it my best. Sometimes when working on the boat, or just cruising around in the harbor, and when it was very smooth, Dad let me sit or lay on the bow of the boat *(like a pretty little hood ornament)* and just watch, or bark (cutely) at the seagulls. Also watch the people on the ships moored in the harbor react to me, and sometime go over and talk to them. When it was time, I always hated to leave, and looked forward to coming back. On the way home we usually ate outside there at a restaurant, so I felt better, because of the harbor view.

When Dad had felt I was old and strong enough, we took short trips on the big "Harley". Dad put me inside his jacket, and when I wasn't sticking my head out to see things or to smell the wind, I slept. <><> Then on one long trip, and where Peaches also came along... leaving early, lots of us... went to the mountains for breakfast... to the desert for lunch... and back to the ocean for dinner... all before nightfall. We stopped often along the way though, because Dad thought I would be too uncomfortable to ride too long at a time (He's thoughtful that way). All the motorcycles would pull off the road for Peaches and me, or anyone else, to stretch, or to "potty". Everyone seemed to enjoy even the stops, because anywhere we stopped on this trip, the scenery was great. Then, from the

"Our" 1974 (Souped-up) Harley"

mountains and the desert, we made our way back to Ventura Freeway. Then up to fabulous Mullholland Drive, where we stopped at a place called "The Rock Store". The owners Ed and Vern were very friendly to me, and always seemed sad to see me go. Sometimes it was there we met other motorcycles riders, with *famous* names like…Arnold, Jay, Sly, Dan, James, Gary and Dwight, and I got petted a lot. We had met some of them at Bartels and had ridden with some. Dad said they were all called "Stars or Celebrities". That sounded important… *but I judged that… by the way they treated Dad and me.*

Leaving there, we headed down toward South Coast Highway. *"Riding along the winding mountain highway, with its beautiful mountain panorama…roaring through a couple of tunnels with throttles open, horns blasting, and 'tops of our voices' yells and screams"*… (I asked Dad to describe that part)… *we arrived at Malibu, and to the peaceful energy of the Pacific Ocean.* We especially enjoyed the beach, where I could run and play, and there were birds and shells and smells to enjoy. Peaches and I played and laughed and got wet and sandy together. We were small enough to even 'fall into a footprint' made in deep loose sand. Such great fun! It was now beginning sunset. So leaving the beach, we always…either stopped at a popular restaurant called "The Fish Place"… or another famous beachside restaurant called "Gladstone's". Both places were good and I certainly *loved the little pieces of fish* (after careful inspection for bones) *for Peaches and me.* So later at home…full, tired and happy…we all slept well that night.

Another place everyone liked to visit on our weekend motorcycle trips, and one I got to go on…most of the time… was up the coast to Santa Barbara. Sometimes, after visiting many of their historical places, we did a little 'hob-knobbing' and visited, and watched, a (horses) Polo Game. Then we went for the fish dinner at a famous restaurant on the pier called Chuck's, (I think). <><><> On another weekend, a beautiful and adventurous trip up South Coast Highway, and then after going over to Solvang, back home through the mountainous lake dotted scenic route…. sure made our day.

Because of Dad's love for Motorcycles and the freedom to ride them…he, Andrea, the local riders of "ABATE." (A Brotherhood Against Totalitarian Enactments), and some other powerful friends, gathered together over "2,000 bikes" (3,000 riders…CHP estimate) and had a rally to protest the passing of a helmet law. Dad and Andrea led it. He wasn't against wearing helmets…"*just a law that would forbid his freedom of choice, to ride with or without one".* I didn't get to go on this ride, but saw it on TV. It looked exciting. Although the law passed anyway… they certainly got their voices heard.

I loved it when we would take his big Harley to Bartel's Harley-Davidson in Culver City (now in Marina Del Rey). Beside the great ride, there and back…Dad loved the noise, the smell of leather, rubber, and gas fumes… as well as, the people we met there. Me too, but I liked better… the pretty girls in the office, who constantly seemed happy to see me, and the warm hugs and little 'doggie treats' they always had for me.

(With *all this traveling around... one night I had a dream...*)

"A COOL RIDE"

"Give me wide-open spaces, winding roads through rolling hills, the wind in my hair... Laughlin ... Sturgis ... Daytona ... here I come!"

Peaches' Mom was a real good singer and musician. Dad sometimes took her to different places to sing and also to 'help her set-up'. He took me...(and sometimes Peaches). Some places he didn't take me... because of the smoke and noise. I got used to the noise...not the smoke. In West Hollywood, one place upstairs called the "Backlot", and downstairs, "The Rose Tattoo", (right around the corner from where she first saw Peaches) she sang and put on her "Show". I went to lots of rehearsals and became acquainted with the staff and many actors. I was in her dressing room a lot and met some folks who also were performing there. I met two females, one called Rosie (O'Donnell), and one called Roseanne (Barr). They seemed to like me. Dad said they were called comediennes and made people laugh and that people feel good when they laugh. He also said these two were good at it... and might even become famous for it. (I liked that, and saw that people usually smiled and laughed at me...so I liked this "Show Business"). There we also met Gary Puckett (*The Union Gap*). Dad said he was 'famous'. He liked Andrea's singing and everyone soon 'hit it off' and became friends. Visiting Peaches', we heard Andrea and him play guitars and sing together. (At one of Gary's party's, I met humans named David Crosby, and a very pretty Morgan Fairchild. She hugged me good, and as she and Dad talked, he seemed...*very happy!* Mostly about me...) (Well...*Of course*)

Andrea also sang at "Carlos and Charlie's" on Sunset Blvd., where she "opened" for Joan Rivers, whom I saw, and also a nice lady...Rita Rudner. Another Club she sang at was "The Gardenia Room". I was getting the... "*Show-Biz-bug'*"

Then Andrea met a famous singer named Luther Van Dross, who heard her sing...liked her... and we all became good friends. They both...Luther and Andrea... had the same Manager, Larry Salvamini... Dad said Larry was famous too. *(Seemed like everybody was "famous" or "a celebrity".)* I didn't understand all about that... but it was fun and Dad seemed happy...so... *"we just let the good times roll".*

For the "*first big*...Aids Benefit", a famous lady named Elisabeth Taylor had a big Press and Publicity "kick off" at the BelAge Hotel. I went too. Andrea was invited to join Elisabeth, Bob Hope, George Hamilton, Linda Ronstadt and the whole cast of the New York Broadway show "Cats"... to sing, and perform at "Lasma Farms" (near Scottsdale, Arizona), famous for its very expensive Arabian horses. (They raised over a million dollars.) Dad was invited and went. Sadly, Peaches or I couldn't, but Dad said he missed me, and even though the event was great, would never want to do that again...without me.

At a place called "Jose' Eber Hair Salon", on beautiful "Two Rodeo", Rodeo Drive, in Beverly Hills... Dad always got his black, 21-inch long hair, "fixed" (dyed and trimmed) by a nice Englishman named Gary. (Jose' is called "The Hairdresser to the Stars" so...where else could we go). Jose' held me... and showed me off... *I liked his hat.* Gary and the staff liked me, and also to carry me around and "show me off". Dad also got 'noticed some', and saw a few "Stars" that *got his attention.* One was actress Susan Blakely. She was very pretty and hugged me good. Dad seemed to really like that...and her. We met her "sweet baby"... **"Harry"** (poodle). Susan was real nice, and with one so kind and sweet, we truly enjoyed ourselves...   *Susan gave us a picture...*

Sometimes we would go early for Dad's appointment. After parking underground, and then riding up on 'the polished brass elevator', and before going upstairs to Jose's; we would walk down the cobble stone street to Rodeo Drive. Folks on the street seemed amazed... and delighted to see me. We always visited the great Shops... Prada, Gucci, Armani, Versace, and Tiffany. (Dad said the movie..."Pretty Woman" was made along here...and...*he smiles at me.*) The folks, who worked there, always greeted us and "made over me" and many gave me treats. (Thus my tea-"*pot*")... We just never knew whom we would meet in these shops. We met several 'local TV and Movie celebrities', and also... "*People from all over the world*"... some who took our picture, and all were very nice.

Earlier, before Jose' moved to Rodeo Drive, his salon was located a few blocks away. It was there we met beautiful actress Victoria Principal, with whom, because of me, Dad had a long conversation. After I received from one so nice...the hugs and customary attention... Dad took over. I was then free to just relax in her lap, or take a nap, or explore the shop. I overheard them talking about her playing a character named

"Pamela" on a TV show called "Dallas", and also manufacturing 'skin care products'. Which however, she didn't seem to need, and because he also had great skin (she mentioned it) I think he was more interested in a "personal demonstration". However…He didn't get one… and I didn't need one… myself being blessed with 'good skin'. When ready to leave, Victoria patted me sweetly and said goodbye. She was very nice…*Dad thought so too.*

Dad had met tons of them before I came, (I had overheard lots of stories) and it would take too long to list all the humans I met, and he says we don't have the time or the room to do so… but these that I met… I just have to mention…*(really… its Him)*

Once while walking on Larrabee Street in West Hollywood, we met Maria Sartis. She was "Counselor Troy, on Star Trek". Dad recognized her… and she stopped and "made over me" for a while. She was very pretty and Dad seemed to want more attention too, but she sweetly said good-bye, and thanked him for letting her pet me. Was that a little sadness I heard in his voice as he said, "you're very welcome" and watched her walk away? So, I guess, "*humans sometimes do feel that helpless rejection*"…even Dads…

Some other folks that we saw or encountered while on our walks, and Dad knew their names… were Paula Abdul, Shaquille "Shack" O'Neil, and Johnny Depp.

One day in the car, just before arriving at a Camera Store on Highland Ave., Dad noticed my signals of discomfort, and turned off on a side street that had lots of grass along the sidewalks. Just before getting back into the car…this caught our attention. We couldn't believe it, but coming around the corner off Highland Ave, was Paula Abdul… recording a video, as she walked along the sidewalk, with a big crew following. We couldn't interrupt her for hugs, but seeing us, she gave us a quick smile. Paula sure looked pretty and sweet…and Dad agreed…we *both* would have enjoyed a warm hug.

Late one afternoon while walking along The Sunset Strip, and as we were just across the street from The Roxy, and The Rainbow Club, two of the popular Nite Clubs there, we saw this great big man that Dad called "Shack", driving a small sports convertible, with the top down. He was stopped across the street and a couple of men got out… Then quickly made a complete U-turn…stopped right in front of us, and smiling broadly and mischievously, got out, stopped the heavy traffic, both ways, and walked back across the street. The two men (bodyguards) whom he had just dropped off, probably got a thrill… or maybe a "chill" thinking how this could have been a big…$$$… tabloid story.

Just up the street on Sunset was Tower Records, where Dad got lots of music, and where once in awhile "famous" singers and singing groups performed outdoors (sometimes on the roof) for very large crowds.. Across the street and right up the hill, was a *famous* restaurant called Spagos, where we parked the car and walked back down to watch the singers at Tower…. *and to see and be seen.* <><><> Because he had once lived in the Windsor Park area, Dad and I loved to visit the trendy stores in Larchmont Village nearby, where many seemed to love us. He had also wanted to lease one of those 5 to 8 bedroom mansions in Hancock Park for us to live in… *didn't happen!*

DAD and ME... *"Happy Days"* My sweet... *"PEACHES"*

One night in West Hollywood, when it was very cold, Dad sneaked me in under his coat, to a place called the Viper Room. And to hear someone called Johnny Depp...play his guitar with his band called "P". Even though the black exterior of the club at the corner of Sunset and Larrabee was a little sinister to me, I had Dad to protect me, and realizing how important "pee-mail" is for "my information" from others, I wanted to see what message I might receive. Besides, Johnny was pretty famous and *'maybe had a cute pet'*. At a break, Dad made me visible to Johnny. He was too surrounded to come over, but saw me and smiled and nodded. Then when they started playing again, they were a little too loud for me, and Dad gestured a goodbye. With a slight smile and body language... Johnny 'waved back'. All these things seemed exciting to Dad, and to them, but I didn't get too excited, as I was too busy enjoying my Dad..."My own superstar", and also "the celebrity of just being my own fabulous self"...Not vanity...just the truth. (Dad smiles... and nods a strong affirmative.)

I didn't mind meeting people, because it made Dad happy. Another means of meeting 'Celebrity humans' was here on Larrabee Street. (Where Dad had lived, and where Peaches and her parents lived now). Pianist-Entertainer Jere Ring (who worked in Las Vegas for Liberace, and now lives in Palm Springs) gave 'elite parties' here on weekends. Jere lived just below us, and soon every one of his five, street-level balconies would be filled with folks and...sometimes where the party...

became accessible to   everyone... even passers-by...

Dad, Tippi Hedren, Andrea (*and Shambala's...*Big Cats)   ...on the sidewalk. As Peaches and I watched them from above, also from one of *our* five wrought-iron balconies, the limousines usually began arriving around 5 o'clock in the afternoon. Things would 'get going' almost immediately and sometimes, some from the "star-studded crowd" would 'spill up' into our apartment...occasionally with *"a cute four-legged cutie"*. Jere's sweet **Logan** (Schnauzer) and us...took every advantage to 'see and be seen'. Everyone had a 'ball'. Oh yes, we also met singer Michael Feinstein, who was staying a few days with Jere, and who we heard sing and play on Jere's "big, black, Grand Piano". Recognizing *'true star quality'* when he saw it, Michael was very nice... to Peaches and me.

On one Sunday, Peaches' and her parents, Dad and I, and that pretty female, Laura, were all invited to the Malibu Beach home of Film Producer Maier Teper. There we also met his friend Arnon Melcher, also a Film Producer ("What's Eating Gilbert Grape") and owner of Regency Films. (Visions of me in movies and on TV swirled around in my head.) Arnon loved to ride motorcycles also, and later made several trips with us. Even though I hadn't met them, or knew their human importance, they were very friendly to everyone and gave me and Peaches the proper amount of adulation and praise that we were fittingly becoming accustomed to. (Dad just smiles as I say this, but he knows it's true). We were also introduced to their friend, and next-door neighbor, Actor Christopher Lambert. Christopher and Dad had a long conversation about a couple of Christopher's many movies, including "Highlander" and " Greystoke"...But mostly... it was about me. (Not surprising!) Later that afternoon some of us, while strolling down the beach... after a great meal, and some great wine (not me, didn't need it), and hearing music and seeing humans having a good time, and they seeing us, we were invited in. It was a birthday party celebration for Sylvester Stallone. He remembered me. (We had met him at The Rock Store, and at Bartels Motorcycles) We accepted their invitation and there, mingled in with some other "Hollywood Stars", I got a great amount of attention. Dad got some too and seemed pleased.   *Happy Birthday Sly!*

Well...you can see by now *that I did go almost everywhere with Dad...* I walked, and explored, and though I was always well behaved...at times he carried me in a 'nice little convertible carrier' (I've asked him to describe some of the places by name).... We went to Shopping Malls (I especially enjoyed The Broadway Center), Hotels (The BelAge and The Mondrian), great Music Concerts in Griffith Park; The Griffith Observatory (many stars); some health food stores (Erewhon, on Beverly Blvd, Wild Oats, in W. Hollywood, Mrs. Gooch's, Beverly Hills). My (our) playground of adventures was truly wide-ranged. From the up-scale shops along Rodeo Drive and after lunch at the Cheesecake Factory, walking and playing in the beautiful park there along Santa Monica Blvd; Great Shops and little "sidewalk" Restaurants (The Old World and The Source) along Sunset Boulevard, where T.V. Producer Stephen J. Cannell gave me an *'on the spot rave review';* And then just for fun, always causing quite a stir among the crowds in front of Grumman's Chinese Theater on Hollywood Blvd. Favorite boutique's and shopping on Melrose Ave, and Santa Monica Boulevard, became our favorite places to walk, and to *see and to be seen*. Also, just below our house in North Hollywood, the fun sidewalks of Universal City. The Santa Monica Pier, 3rd St. Promenade, and the great many little shops there. Several cities also in Orange County: Two trips to Disney in Anaheim and especially to... Manhattan

Beach, Huntington Beach and Newport Beach. The South Coast Plaza, Balboa, Palos Verdes, Marina Del Rey, Laguna Beach and Laguna Niguel, were all just too pretty to not visit and play in...and there were even more.

Finally...This I have to tell, and though it may sound strange to some humans... quite understandable to others, ...but my first (and last) trip to the Griffith Park Zoo left me so very sad. Dad understood my feelings, but even after he explained some of the good they do for some animals, and that so many humans enjoyed... *the sight of them in bondage... behind bars or in cages... all out of their normal habitat... and then our communications... and hearing and feeling their pain of confusion... and longing to be free...*left me very sad. I would never forget it.

There are so many stories about the adventures and the beautiful humans I have met and that I have not mentioned. However, Dad says I have talked a lot and have to go for now and rest, but that I can come back soon and write more about my adventures in "Gracie's World."   So...Good night all, ...Gracie

<><><>

Sometimes things happen in the human world that changes their lives... and ours. Dad's life drastically changed financially, and we moved. I hated to leave there, but as long as I was with Dad, I knew things would be OK. We moved to Martha Street in Van Nuys, for about a year. It was a beautiful, smaller, two-bedroom house...(About the size of our last living room and kitchen). However it was fenced-in all around, had a great front and back yard, and lots of flowers and grass and some fruit trees. Dad even planted a garden, and I helped...*with some digging*. The garden brought in lots of tomatoes and other things and we shared them with the neighbors. We still had lots of visitors, and also made lots of friends with the neighbors, so we were happy there.

Then things changed again, and for a short while, we moved in with Peaches and her parents. Even though it was wonderful being with Peaches, I had hated to move again... but Dad knew best.

Then something *else* happened... Dad had an appointment of some kind in Sherman Oaks. In the waiting room (which I promptly took over) we met and talked to a very attractive and very friendly female human...(Dad's favorite kind it seemed). Anyway, to make a long story short, her mother, whom she described as very pretty (Dad is listening even closer now) and living in another city, was having problems (even suicidal) with a failed relationship and would Dad (a minister) visit her and counsel her. Then after a 3 day trip to Palm Springs (without me if you can believe it) to meet the woman who was having a bad time and needed some 'personal counseling', he came back and got me... and then began....

Our New World... In Palm Springs

Moving to Palm Springs, new and different adventures began immediately.

On thing... Dad said they didn't have many fleas here, so I was happy about that. On South Sunrise Way, we rented a private room and bath from a nice (and pretty) female human, named Donna. She loved animals. She had three beautiful "children"... **Mary** (a Bichon), **Darling** (a Shitzu) and **Lonnie** (a Bichon)...we got along well. So did she and Dad...*very well*... (Sometimes, Dad even had dinner ready for her). We lived in a place called a Country Club, surrounded by beautiful grounds and with acres of green grass and trees. Every morning Dad and I explored for a couple of hours and met people, dogs, ducks, birds, and sometimes a rabbit or squirrel. I liked the bridge overlooking the small lake and where we could watch the ducks and the fish.

Donna...*My Groomer.*

Donna owned "Puppy Luv", a Grooming Salon downtown, where I enjoyed getting pretty (er)...and began to meet some of her "special customers". (They were all special to her). ...Frank Sinatra's, fifteen (15) "babies"... among them for ten years.. Sadly I didn't get to meet them, or they me. Another special one was Jasmine or **"Jazzy"** (a Bichon Frise) whose parents were Penny and Dr. Earl Mason. (Dr. Mason played jazz on his trumpet hence her name.

My new friends... *pretty* **Mary**, *and sweet* **Jazzy**

Donna, **Dahling**, and Me, *at LeVallauris*

Zsa Zsa, and *Dahling's Daddy*

Donna, who groomed some of the Gabor's "babies", introduced us to Magda Gabor. We visited her beautiful Palm Springs home several times and were introduced to her five "precious darlings". One of them was also named **Darling** ("Dahlink"...in 'Gabor') who would later live with Donna. Donna said Magda was perhaps the most beautiful of all, was very smart and spoke several languages. She liked me lots...and *I sure understood that language.* Several times she took me into her clothes closet and it seemed big enough for us all to live in... it was filled to the top of its 'twelve ft. ceiling' with double tiers of clothes and coats and shoes and some red hats...they were pretty... sadly none fit me. Donna said that Jolie "Mama" Gabor, Magda, and her sisters, Eva and Zsa Zsa... loved to frequent LeVallauris Restaurant and their center table in the Garden. Magda loved to wear red, and a red hat, and became famous for it.

Some time later, Magda became very ill. And though I couldn't go, Dad and Donna visited her at Eisenhower Hospital, where sadly, she passed away. On one visit, *she had asked about me.* Dad was so emotionally moved by it, that after Magda's death, he started taking me to visit people in hospitals, geriatric and pediatric wards, and those in Retirement Homes. We also became well acquainted with the nurses and some staff at Eisenhower Hospital and many at Desert Hospital, where we were welcomed to make our visits. Beginning with this, we not only got the reward of helping others, but our reputation got public attention. Even though we knew that I could have 'a special effect' on humans, Dad and I both were sometimes amazed and elated at the 'immediate effect' our visits had on the patients, and the stories of the 'lingering effects', that were quite possibly a great part in helping to heal and expedite their recovery. We also soon found how very concerned the Coachella Valley was about the welfare of animals ...and that there were lots of good folks, doing lots of good things... for both.

Often when certain events would happen and I would see Dad's reaction, I would think of those words Mom had told me when I was young...about "us being another nation and hearing words they never hear". *I believed Dad did hear those voices...because he believed they existed, and could help our work.* Dad's had "a short fuse" in dealing with those guilty of cruelty toward any animal, and could be easily provoked, not just to anger, but also to action. And it was not unusual for him to confront anyone he thought was abusing one, especially leaving their pet in a hot car, or on the hot floor of an open bed pickup truck in summer. I saw him do it, and he didn't seem at all afraid. (I might add...he felt the same about 'human abuse'....) Also, when reading about it, or seeing things about it on television (I loved to watch TV, too)...and when he felt that I could take it, Dad told me of some of the things that many animals, of all kind, suffer every day, and usually at the hands of humans. I could hardly believe it. I had never gone hungry, been mistreated, kept in a cage, or been cold and deserted, so I could only imagine how it must be for some of my brothers and sisters. I cried for them. Dad and I dedicated our time and efforts to help eliminate as much suffering as possible for... animals and humans. Dad said every bit ...large or small, helps. He was right.

Donna introduced us to a 'special' man named Bob Howard. He seemed to really like me, and invited us to his home. I can only say, "this was an adventure I'll never forget". Dad either. Bob had two homes, across the street from each other. Showing his knowledge of "from insects to mammals"...Both houses was filled with 'memorabilia'. There were 'stuffed' images of animals and reptiles (and some alive) from all over the world. (I stayed in Dad's arms for this tour). Bob did research and founded the "Big Horn Institute" to help preserve the Big Horn sheep of the Coachella Valley and elsewhere. He told us the touching story of "**Howard**", the first-born lamb at the Institute and named after him. I would love to have met him. Bob did great work to preserve these magnificent and peaceful animals. I was quite impressed with him, and the visit.

Another of Donna's customers and friends was Ruthie Patencio. Ruthie was an American Indian and really liked me. She liked limousines. One year she invited us to a Thanksgiving dinner at someone's house where there were lots of other Indian folks and the house was rich in Indian culture. Dad seemed very interested in all this, because he said he was also part "Cherokee Indian". All I know is that they were kind to me and the house smelled of good food. (This time Dad fed me a little more turkey than usual, and so I began to understand a little more about what Thanksgiving *really* means).

<><><><>

After almost two years, and thinking everything was fine at "our house", even though "once in awhile, there were some pretty tense moments between them"...(I don't think it was just Dad's cooking) well, anyway... Dad and I moved out. I missed everybody. I missed Mary, Darling and Lonnie. I missed Donna. It was sad. (Thankfully, we soon began visiting each other, and this made things much better)

Dad and I moved into an "Alexander style house" on Starr Road in north Palm Springs (and would live there for almost five years). After awhile I got used to it, and settled in. We went walking every morning in the neighborhood, and then to the beautiful Victoria Park nearby. Many times there we met a very friendly man, also walking, named Ron Oden. Dad said he was a Councilman for the city, but talked about running for Mayor, and Dad said he probably would. He was very kind to me and petted me, and we would all walk together for a little while. I really liked this park.

Because I wanted to help everyone enjoy his or her life, even more, I had thought for some time about writing. Rick Cherry suggested the weekly, Desert Daily Guide. (Going to 25 cities in 12 States). I began writing...(with Dad's help), the weekly page article ..."Ask Gracie". It was intended to focus on Animal Rights and answer questions from readers about their pets and their problems. However, because so many interesting things were happening in my life, and I was becoming involved with so many local events, it soon developed into more of a weekly "Gracie's Society Page". It became quite popular and according to many opinions, took on a kind of *'cult following'*. I got letters and Emails. I wrote 52 articles for them. Dad was proud of me...and that made me happy. Then...I had an adventure at home, which made me have to write about it in two of my articles. Dad said I should... so here they are... just the way I wrote them...

Hello Sweethearts...

I had an experience I would like to share with you, one that tested most of the fibers and cells in my body. The ones that didn't get tested were hiding somewhere too shook-up to come out. Maybe I'm making it sound too scary...but you be the judge. You that have been through something like this will understand and the rest of you can only surmise. You know how dedicated I am to this Animal Rights program, overall, and will do literally anything to advance its progress, yet...I had to deal with something I had never dealt with. Dad says humans have to deal with similar circumstances during their lives and have to learn from their experiences. Now...Dad and I are inseparable and share everything, our lives, our time, our adventures, our thoughts...everything that a human and *us* can experience together. Could anything come between us...? Well...here's what happened. A week ago when Dad went into the back yard, for something, I heard him using endearing tones, toward something. I immediately ran to investigate and there...in our yard...close to my Dad...even being coaxed...was a CAT. Every DNA strand, of centuries of breeding, rushed to my head...and feet...and the attack was on. I didn't even stop to think at that moment what Dad would think...I only knew my territory...our territory...was being invaded and Dad needed protecting. (At least this was the excuse I would use later, but right now I didn't 't have time to explain.) Seeing me... the cat bolted...I barked...and Dad yelled. I was feeling pretty good about it all, until Dad registered a bit of annoyance. He hugged and petted me and explained that he understood my reaction, but that I needed to follow his lead the next time the cat returned. *The next time! The Cat returned!* ...We didn't need a cat... or anything else...we were a Secure Unit of Animal Rights...a Team for Animal Rights...a Voice of Animal Rights! Then I saw a smile and a twinkle in Dad's eyes and I knew... I had just come face to face... *with a real life example of...Animals Rights.*

Dad fed the cat for a week (it was pretty skinny). It gained weight...refused to run from me...and was there every morning... and every night... and slept on the porch! When he thought that she (yes...it was a she) was strong enough, we took her to Animal Samaritans to have her "spayed". (Dad took her in "My" nearly new... airline approved, zippered and accessorized, convertible flight carrier) And brought her back, the same way and the same day. I could imagine... *that spaying visit* was quit a shock to her...but she's doing fine ... and I'm getting 'a bit more' used to her. I still have Dad, and nothing has changed with our love. I've learned, first hand...the feeling of" "rights for animals and humans. Dad says he's proud of me! Now I'm growing...and a little smarter. Love Gracie XXXOOO   P.S. ... Dad named her **"Misty"**

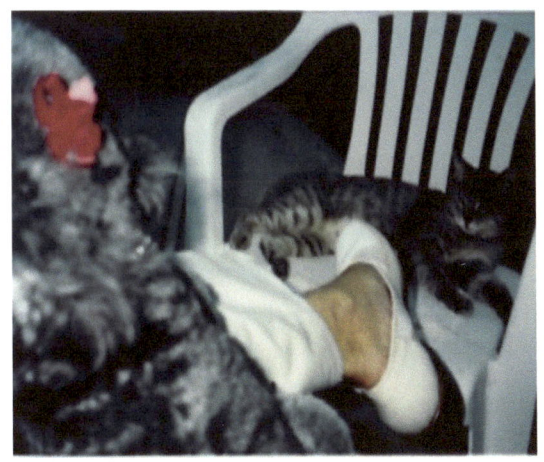 

Yep... *That's her...*   Dad...*is this picture really necessary... Meow"*

(Second article)... Hello Sweethearts...

This has been a week of self-examination. Yes, Misty is still here. She's recuperating nicely thank you...getting stronger, healthier (fatter) and well, yes...even friendlier. However...yesterday when I got too close to her food, she gave me a little swat at with her paw. The nerve! She didn't fully extend her claws though, so the only damage... was to my pride. She says she wants to be friendly, yet she still hisses and growls slightly and says, "get away" when I get too close. Maybe we should both 'chill' a little.

To make my life a little more complicated...now... there are *two cats*. Another one Dad calls **"Boots",** who has been showing up every day for a meal, which Dad never hesitates to give. There's also a little petting and scratching demands... that Dad also supplies. Will it never end? Is this the diminishing of my reign as "the Apple of Dad's eye?" This thought came crashing into my senses, but was quickly dispelled when Dad said, "Lets go for a ride, baby" and we were off in the car... towards new adventures.   It's these rides in the car, the people we visit and see in the hospitals, and downtown in the shops, the restaurants, and all my friends...that make *"even the Cats"* worthwhile. (Smile) I think I even like the cats. Never thought I would say that, but teaching makes you understand, even your enemies...which now, they aren't anymore.

So, after some... '*Close inner-prospective proliferations and effervescent effeminate evaluations'*...my conclusion is... *"I am still The Quintessential Queen of Smiles, The Desert Diva of Desire, Lady of Unreserved Adoration and Poise, and of indisputable Humility,"* (So...try that on for size..."Misty and Boots"!) Dad says there is nothing like... *genuine humility...* So, here I am *"Sufficiently Humble"* ... Love, Gracie xoxoxo

<><>   <><>

Dad spoiled me with good things. (Not spoiled...just deserving) To see that I was healthy, and ate well, he ordered in *by mail, from Harbor City, CA.*, a special frozen "raw meat and vegetable " combination. Also supplements. Always-fresh reverse-osmosis filtered water.

He brushed me almost every morning (Even Diva's can have a bad hair day), and always, before, and after, a bath. He brushed my teeth, , and little stairs to get up on the bed. When we had to be outside in summer, he always picked me up when the sidewalks were hot, or anytime I asked him...Never left me in the car...Always-fresh bottled water

... Just so many little things he did... I loved my Dad. So when he taught me several tricks, I was always glad to oblige...even without treats. Oh yes, and I still got my scheduled grooming at Donna's. And because of her unique way of doing it...my "Special-for-Gracie-Teddy-Bear-Cut"...I soon became the talk of downtown Palm Springs, especially on Palm Canyon and Indian Avenue. With our "year-round-nice-weather", we stayed busy.

"Ready for Palm Canyon"

Sometimes little crowds would gather and car horns would blow for us. *There is little that gives a girl more pleasure... than to see and be seen...and to bring you those moments of satisfaction... and in ways only we can do it!* (Dad is nodding in agreement).

<><><>   Street Scenes   <><><>

"I was always on top *doing this"*

"Dad...I think this rock just moved"

Visiting sweet **"Toi"** *at...Dani-C's*

"Street Vibrations"   ...indeed

"Sweet Sue" ...*WE, sweet or what!*

Friends from Canyon Lake, CA

"Thanks Dad, nice picture of...HER"

Sarika, Me, and Dr. Lawrence Ramalho

With Stephanie & **"Pillsbury"**...
At Starbucks

"Busted"... by Officer Palmer...
"Under the influence...dealing in smiles"

Katie Me **Mary** Jazzy P.AW.S. Pres, Rick Cherry and Me,
(Top) John, Penny Mason, Donna, Dr. Earl Mason   and Rick Empie ...

Three *"cool"* models at Givenchy   *"V-Twin"... Memories*

"Cool"... and The Gang   *"Waiting for Dad... and my helmet? "*

"Craig...I'm available for films"

Bruce, Joey, Wayne, & me..."Up town"
"Oh yes...scratch right there"

" Dad... maybe a little smaller beret?"

Holding me for Ransom

"Miss Harley-Davidson, 2001"

Ken Dawson and...*three*... pretty girls

Kay Sachs and Me... *"Stylin"*

Linda Christian and me..."*We cool*"

Hey Dad...*that's the 10th picture!*

Mary Ann Mott, *"pretty"*, good writer

Grace, Me, Dick, Joey, and Phil

Alan Keller... *"Tommy-Too's"* Dad

Margaret & **George**, Elaine & me...   That's me *"in the green"* at Givenchy

..."*Picture of lovin*"

At the Street Fair...*resting with my friend...* **"Hoss"**

Andy Fraga...*Sunday's at Melvyn's*   Denise... *"Gourd Artist"*...I'm next!

Jackie Olden, *Cooking Show (Yumm)...*

Michelle gave me water... *& Luv*

Jean Soich...*A sales purrrrson*

Twin hugs..."*doubles the pleasure*"

"Daddy Bear" Edward...

P.A.W.S Easter Charity...

Dennis Stevens, owner

(Pets Are Wonderful Support)

Sharon Hougen...*sweet, loved me--* "*Pretty*" Diane...She said... *I was too!*
and her daughter Heidi ...*loved me too.*

Josh and Joan Joseph...sweet humans   Ken Prescott...Broadway...Sings...
(They loved Jazz...and me)   Nice hair... *(Smelled good too)*

Hilda & Thad...*where video was made.*   Juan, Nina and J.B. (Bork's Shoes)

Though (sadly) Dad had cut his long hair, and began to wear it 'conventional'... he still liked to look good. By this time, he had also found a "personal groomer" that he liked,  and he started going to Sharon Petrilla, "to keep him looking pretty". I liked to go there too, as she was pretty, and liked me, and everyone there was very friendly. After I would make my visits to each chair (to get, my 'happy fix') they laughed... at the way I sometimes 'sprawled on the floor' to keep my belly cool, and to wait for Sharon to "do her magic" on Dad. He always seemed very pleased with the results. So did I.

Sharon... *"Dad's Groomer"*

"Guess who took this one"...   Bill Farrell *looks onto..."My Paradise"*

Pres. Mike Russell (far right) & friends.   *Now where is my Baton?*

We wanted to expand our effectiveness in 'doing good'. As we became better known in the community, our efforts got us the attention of Animal Samaritans ASPCA in Thousand Palms. We contacted the Director of Public Relations, Dick Williams… (Also the Dad to five "boys", including Beauty (black Lab) and Earl (American Eskimo)… with

our request to help. Meeting Mike Russell, the President of Animal Samaritans, we were invited to a Holiday Luncheon, honoring Jim and Jackie Lee Houston as "Humanitarians of the Year". (That got our attention) That "sweet human lady" (I just love to refer to her this way) Jackie Lee was so kind and was very loving to me and later even sent me 'stationery, made with her and my picture together on it'. She was always dressed pretty and Dad said she had once been a "Top 10 Fashion Model" (I believed she still was). Dad said she did many things to help animals. He

Sweet…"Jackie Lee and Mee"   said she and her husband Jim (He liked me too) were also very much involved in helping humans. My heart was really full that day…and so was Dad's.

We also met Pamela Green…a real sweet human, a strong supporter of Animal Samaritans, and a good mom to several **"furry feline children"**. She liked us, and would become a close friend…(Especially…in time to come). Her husband, Irving "Irv" Green, famous for founding Mercury Records and building houses… would also become a good friend. She was pretty, and was always "groomed" so nice… so naturally I felt really close to her.

At that luncheon, I was awarded the title "Roving Reporter". Dad helped me write some stories for their quarterly publication…"Animal Tales." Dad and I handed out hundreds of business cards for Animal Samaritans… with my picture on them, to the folks on the streets in downtown Palm Springs, Palm Desert, and just anywhere else we could, …encouraging the "spaying and neutering" of their animals, and for their next pet… to also "think seriously, about adopting a rescued shelter animal". Seldom did anyone who met us or made a comment about me, not receive a card and a verbal encouragement from Dad. We had a happy feeling, and anticipated that this was doing some good. Some said we were responsible for thousands of dollars being donated. Marie George, Director (who liked us both) introduced us to Paulette Mullinax, Animal Samaritans Director of Education. Through her, we also visited a school. This way we could talk to a 'big bunch at a time' and have a more informed effect on them and their families.

Visiting the Agua Caliente School...*Great fun.*   Nursing Home visit...*(check our coloring)*

Joan "Jonie" Helgesen was known as the "Swan Lady", for her untiring efforts to save the beautiful swans that occupied and nested in some of the "Country Club" lakes in the valley. We were invited to her home and to make the rounds in her boat and see the beautiful black, and white swans. Kate Porter made some video for her TV program.

"Winkle"... *Joni and me ...*

Top: (l. to r.) **Bentley** and **Princess**

Dad and I often visited a Ladies Apparel shop called The Wardrobe. **Sharon** (Jacobs) was so nice to us and had four sweet beauties that we both couldn't resist visiting most every time we went downtown. Dad said Bentley was like the *"Eveready Bunny"* in the energy department...but sweet. I agreed.

Bottom: **Taddy** and **Buffy**

Lori Sarner is President of The Pegasus Riding Academy...where...they do such a great work for handicapped children and adults of all ages ...with horses and their "Equine Therapy" (I always admired the beauty and strength, and yet the gentleness these huge animals...and wanted to get closer, but Dad said I best just look for now). Lori was a very busy woman, however she and husband Harvey always had time to be sweet and friendly to Dad and me. (I may yet get to go there and meet some of those big wonderful horses...and some of the children).

Lori and **"Rocket"**...*one love of her life*

Dad and I also met **Sandy Benson** and her husband **Ron**. Sandy was a nice lady, the Mom to **"Brandelle"** her beloved (miniature Schnauzer), and a big supporter of Animal Samaritans. Sandy always seemed to be in demand as an organizer for many of their charitable events. We visited her home a couple of times and I got hugged...and even though Brandelle watched somewhat jealously, I understood, and we made friends.

Sandy... *a picture of love...to remember*

Pegasus Riding Academy and Animal Samaritans team up every year for a "Pets on Parade" to raise funds. I always attended with Dad. The first year, Dad submitted my picture, and I won one of the "Runner- Up" awards. Then...California Seniors had a contest and I was chosen "The Grand Champion Winner". Later...we attended the IABCA...International All Breed Canine Association of America, Inc. Dog Show (whew) at Ruth Hardy Park and (because "tea-cups" ain't recognized for show") won a certificate (a #2 Red Ribbon) for participating. But unofficially, they awarded me a "Blue Ribbon for Cutest Pet" at the show.

So...we were getting around, and I was winning a few contests. Good for my image...and my self-esteem. (...And Dad's)

The Shitzu won "*First*"...and...*ME !*

Hey Dad...*Look how strong I am*

We got a phone call, inviting us to an "animal related" fundraiser in Palm Desert. Dad invited "my sweet Lindi Biggi", and so we met her there. Cris DeRose from Los Angeles, a former Actor, now Animal Activist and Author of the book "IN YOUR FACE", was in town. The book is about his effective activities to close down those (heartless and corrupt) "puppy mills" and also the numerous... (Equally corrupt) Federally Licensed "pet-theft mills". Cris heads a group called "Last Chance for Animals" (LCA) who gather evidence against, and "bust these pet-theft perverts"...who buy from newspaper advertisements, or just steal your household pets out of your yard, and sell them *for heartless vivisection experiments*. He showed a movie of puppy mills. It was too hard to watch it all. We came away...sad for the victims...angry with the perverts...but happy for Cris. We certainly need many more serious warriors like Cris... and his people.

Guide Dogs of The Desert International, located on Dillon Road in Whitewater, who does such a fabulous service for the Blind, created a 9-category awards program called "The Arf-Academy Awards", to honor canine participants, their "parents" and to raise funds. At their first one, I was invited to be an "Honorary Presenter". I did, and *Dad helped*. It was held at their auditorium, and was a fun time for all Canines and Humans. Afterward, I communed with some of my *beautiful brothers and sister* that they call **"guide dogs"**... "I fell in love several times that night."

Even though the cement sidewalks could really mess up my (red) manicured nails, Palm Canyon was one of our favorite places to walk and show them off. (At Xmas time, Donna painted them. red and green... or silver...or sometimes even gold... *Mercy*!) I never needed a leash. I listened to Dad. I learned early that 'curbs are boundaries' and to cross streets only when Dad does. Sidewalks were (mostly) safe...streets dangerous. Like I said...listen to Dad. We only used a leash when Dad felt I would need protection, or to conciliate some good rule.

Janet Newcomb caught us ..."*Out on the Town*"!

Once, when seeing me on Palm Canyon without a leash, and not immediately identifying me being with Dad, her uncontrollable urge to rescue me, resulted in us meeting and making long lasting friends with Sally and Randy Largent (snow bunnies...er...birds) from Seattle. They also had a "furry sweetie" named **Keiki** that they had to leave at home in Washington, and were by now "*really*" missing

Randy & Sally... *"My Seattle friends"*

Desmonds Men Store was a friendly place to visit. I really appreciated their love... and the little "dog's head" water fountain outside that was always ready to give others and me a cool drink. Also it was there; among several people crowded around us listening to Dad tell about me, that Dad saved my life. Dad spotted a big Kia and it's human coming down the street. He felt danger. Sure enough, slipping through the people, the Kia grabbed me. I felt pain... but then... felt me flying through the air. Dad had kicked it so hard, that I went flying, as we were propelled backward. I was frightened, but not hurt badly. Donna treated me. After the shock, and relieved that I was all right, Dad felt kinda bad...the Kia was hurt I'm sure, but it was necessary to do. (I had little sympathy)

Donna was a member of the Palm Springs Chamber of Commerce, and invited us to be her guest. We enjoyed it. Dad decided that I should attend more meetings. We did and I became a "dues paying member" of the Chamber of Commerce. Through this, we met lots of people and Dad gave out lots of our "spay and neuter" cards. We met the CEO David Aaker and Bill Casey and others that were all extra friendly. The Chamber of Commerce had it 60th Anniversary and we were invited. They had lots of food and stuff and lots of balloons. As you can see... people thought it funny when I ran around with a few of them tied to my collar. *One more balloon, and I'd be off to the moon...*

The Palm Springs Chamber had many events and at one of their Expos we set up a little booth just to "give out some smiles". Many businesses were represented and we saw lots of our friends among them and also among the public. One special one was little Juliann Nichole Stiny who was "Little Miss Americas-Universe International 2000". We swapped "pointers on being queens". We both got lots of attention that day.

Many of our friends, including Elaine, lived in Palm Desert. We *"did El Paseo"* often. In this beautiful and affluent setting...we liked to cruise the sidewalks and great stores there and watch the many smiling expressions on faces. There we met TROY, a special Lady, and her two (Bichon) "fur kids"...**Dolly** and **Missy**. Troy liked me lots.

Troy and Penny...*Shining bright on El Paseo...*

Also on Palm Canyon, we met Roger and Karen Connell and their little sweetheart **"Munchkin"**, who was sweet, very cute, and…even smaller than me. We loved to play at the Palm Springs Doggie Park.

Munchkin"…*Little, and loveable*

We always seemed welcome in all the shops. At a Dress Shop called "DANI-C", the pretty owner, talked 'love' to me in her French accent, and had a cutie pie 'Shitzu' named **"Toi"**. Thus were the incentives for our frequent visits. We made lots of sweet friends that way.

"Toi", Dani-C (French lady) & Me

<><> Sometimes our walking companions, on Palm Canyon and at other events, were famous Sculptor, Colin Webster-Watson and **Andrew** (Pekingese). Seeing some of Colin's amazing (Bronze) sculpture, I thought…*what an honor it would be…to be 'bronzed' by an artist so gifted, and whose art is so sensually perceptive.* <><>

"Marcel… was one man that literally 'rolled out the carpet' for me…a striking man, who owned Marcel De Claremont Rug Gallery Inc. He dressed real sharp, and liked me, so… he, Dad, and I… got along real well.

On Marcel's (red) carpet"

At Kabotine …one of those little shops, where this

pretty girl took a picture of me, then Dad took one of and her and me, and it turned out so good he got the idea of keeping a photo album.

At Sam Bork's 'popular' shoe store on Palm Canyon, we met friendly **Sam Bork**, sitting outside. It was there…after seeing a grown man, in a suit, lying on the floor, playing with me…and Dad wishing for a camera, "he never went without one again". Earlier, he had also missed one of Mayor Kleindienst, *on his hands and knees in his office, playing a game with me.* He later got a picture of the Mayor and me when we attended an Easter party.

And where we also, met and got a sweet picture with TV Talk Show Host Gloria Greer, the mom of her beloved **"Sam Greer"** (Lhasa Apsa). That day, Gloria and I had on matching pink.

Gloria and Me... *"Pretty in Pink"*

In Sam Bork's Shoe Store, I was kissed, hugged by, and gave a kiss to, beautiful Cathy Lee Crosby. It was great, and Dad got the picture...(and that's all he got ...*hee hee*).

Cathy Lee... *" Biding my time..."*   *"GOTCHA"*

Marianne's Dress Shop (formerly "Fitzgerald's") was where we met Marianne Hunnzinger and her whole 'crew'. She and Dad became...very good friends. She especially liked me, and once in awhile, even cooked some great dinners for us, at her home. Marianne's "true love" (for 20 years)... was a beautiful and very personal... Siamese cat named **"Saby"**... However, she made some room in her heart for me and...also for Dad.

Marianne *loved me...very much*

Dear Editor   (Email)

Gracie is the most wonderful ambassador on Palm Canyon! Little precious Gracie puts the smile into everyone's heart; even the unfriendliest people start smiling. God bless her and her dad. We love Gracie's and her very nice Dad's visits to our store.

The Girls from Fitzgerald's—

    Marianne, Jennifer, Cindy, Ruth, and Bob too!

"Floor exercises" at Marianne's...

A Patriotic moment with Mary...

Dad and I made several trips "upstairs" (when it was) on Palm Canyon, to Congresswoman Mary Bono's office. There, a nice lady named Anne Bryant always greeted us and would tell Mary we were there. Dad said Mary had a big job, with something called 'the government', and so, she was important. We had our picture made together, and with the American Flag (which Dad says is also important) in the background. We always enjoyed our visits and always came away "feeling a little more Patriotic".

In front of the St. James Restaurant, on Palm Canyon, we met and got a great picture of Val and Yolande Donlan Guest. He a British film director and she an actress... with their darling "Mischa"... a poodle, and so black, she is hard to see in the picture. Dad liked those very sharp 'ascots' Val wore, and Val promised to bring him some from London on his next trip. Dad said he would like to take me there someday. Hey...anywhere Dad goes...I am ready.

Val, "Mischa", Yolanda, and Me.

Health Food Stores were always on our "good will" route. Lisa and Spencer (also animal lovers) at Nature's RX on Sunrise, was where we always got good hugs, good things, and a hug from Patti. When I would feel poorly, Lisa would give me some herbs and also a big hug to make me feel better. <><> Another one we also loved to visit was Oasis Health Foods, on Indian Ave. where we also got food and supplements, and where owner Diane Weeks hugged us, as did many of her customers... I'm not sure which kept us healthier, the food or the hugs.

(I have to say though, sometimes I felt... for my health's sake, Dad really didn't want so many people hugging me, and sometimes, he politely refused strangers. However, knowing how "irresistible" I was, and because it was part of my "profession", and also when he saw I really wanted to, he felt ok to allow it for a short time, and even then... he was always close to take me back when I was ready.)

Some of the Restaurants in Palm Springs graciously gave Dad and me 'special privileges', some, with a private table. Harold Matzner, the owner of Spencer's Restaurant and a special friend to animals, always came over to our table to welcome us, and sometimes with his handsome **Spencer** Matzner (Siberian Husky). (Even Spencer's head... was bigger than me!)

The owners of "Cedar Creek Inn", Frederick and Desiree' Gerhardt, and Laura Lee, the head hostess, always had a special table on the patio for us, and everyone seemed to like it when we came into the restaurant.

And even though we didn't have a special table, at either the Palm Springs or the Palm Desert "Native Foods Restaurants", the owner Tonya, always greeted us and acted glad to see us. Dad liked to eat healthy. These were both good places to do it. *Tonya, Native Foods...yummy.*

Once after a visit to the one in Palm Desert, we walked across El Paseo, where I played in the grass at a place called The Gardens. Then to Saks, where outside we had a chance meeting with two ladies. Dad called one Jane (Wyman). He later said she had been a great movie actress and was once married to a man named President Reagan ...This all sounded very impressive, but the loving way she hugged and made over me... *told me all I needed to know.*

Your White House Buddy 🐾

The Givenchy Restaurant and Spa, owned (then) by **Merv Griffin**, provided us with a special table, and for months was our favorite Sunday noon destination. I met Merv only once. He was charming and gave me a warm hug and said I was especially cute... and then with a grin... asked if I had met **Charlie Chan** (his Sharpei). After that I always hoped to see Charlie there, but I never did.

Although Dad had earlier written to **President Bill Clinton** in Washington, D.C. telling him about me, and the President, probably hopeful for his (chocolate Lab) Buddy 's chances with me, sent us this picture ... Nevertheless because I was 'playing the field'... and **Buddy** was 'up there' in Washington... I still looked for Merv's handsome (a great personality... and "beauty is in the eye of the beholder") boy, Charlie Chan...and although our affections could only be ...*platonic*, I dug this *'suitors competition thing'*.)

I met and got hugged by many local talents... Ruth Gibson, Rick Marlow, Helen G, Phil and Grace Moody, Bill Farrell, Stephanie Phillips, Richard Johnson, and sometimes out of town guests, who preformed on weekends at Merv's Givenchy and Spa <><> Bill Marx (fabulously) played the piano, for all the singers, and always "announced my entrance" into the room. He even played "chopsticks" with my paws at the piano. He was sweet to me. So were Bill's beautiful wife Barbara and their beautiful "babies...**Cappuccino and Maestro**". Barbara always hugged me...good. We first met her at The LeVallauris, and got this fab picture.

Bill Marx... *"Chopsticks anyone?"*   Barbara Marx & Me, *"giving love"*

It was here that I first met "famous" singer and movie actor, Herb Jeffries, who believe it or not, is even 'older than Dad'...(giggle.) Dad said he saw him in a western movie when he (Dad) was just a young boy. Some said he and Dad looked like brothers. His wife Savannah was nice and Dad seemed specially to like her Southern name. (Dad had been born in a place called... Georgia). <><> Then one Sunday we met Tony Bennett, who Dad said was an extra famous singer. He didn't sing that day. Dad asked if we

Tony ... "He left his heart..."

Tony and Herb, "I'm seein Stars"...

could ...he said sure...so we got pictures together. He hugged me real good...(and he smelled good too). Then Herb Jeffries came over and we got another picture of the three of us together. <><> "Talk of the Town", Show Host Melinda Read, (who dad said had once won a "Mrs. California International" beauty contest) was there and held me real good and we got another good picture. Her husband Tom, whom I remember had a real deep voice and was real kind to me, was there too, but somehow he didn't get into the picture. <><>

Melinda Reed & me... "At Givenchy"

Bill and Barbara... "making my day"

Artist and designer Elaine Murphy, whom we had met a week earlier, and her real pretty mother Ilene, from Dublin, Ireland, were there and we hugged and talked. They were 'very pretty'; Dad seemed particularly interested... *but loved me even better...*

Elaine and Me...*at Givenchy*

Mom... Ilene ..."*a good Irish hug*".

All the *"long-legged beauties"* from The Palm Springs Follies were there for lunch one Sunday, and Dad and I "worked the room"...Again lots of pictures, and some great ones with them and me, around the piano with Bill.

Bill, Me, & ... "*WOW*"

Leila & me...*we stylin'!*

Leila, Me, Dorothy and Roz

Stephanie and Me, at Givenchy

<><> Once, right in the middle of someone's song, actor Sean Connery and a friend, strolled slowly through the room, not stopping, but glancing our way as he went out the door to the garden, causing quite a 'twitter' among the gals and even some of the guys. Dad said he was famous. He must have been... because he got 'almost as much attention as me'. I wondered if he might have a **"sweet fuzzy four-legged love"** at home. Didn't find out. <><> There we met Gino Lamont, and actor Fred (*The Hammer*) Williamson and his wife Linda. Got a picture! Gino had heard about my new "expensive necklace" that I had just received from an anonymous admirer, so he invited Dad and me to appear on his KMIR-6 TV program to talk about it. It sure was pretty around my neck on TV... and you know how I love to *'style!*

Fred, and wife Linda...and us.   KMIR 6...Gino, all about my *"bling"*.

Later, when I appeared on KESQ Channel 3, with Dick Williams for Animal Samaritans, "Pet Adoptions", Ginger Jeffries the "weather Girl" gave me some 'warm weather' hugs and Dad was there with his trusty camera. For many of these events, Barbara Barnett had given me a great 'carrier', with little pink hearts on it. We were styling.

Dick, April, and Todd..."TV3"   KESQ Ginger... *"fair skies"*.   Barbara & *my new ride*

(During these years, it would be almost impossible to tell of the things that would most affect Gracie's life, and the lives that she would most affect. However, considering time and space, we can but try to capture some of them…David)

As you can tell, Dad believed we should be involved in the many human activities in the Valley and I agreed. I was invited to and really enjoyed many ceremonies in downtown Palm Springs for "The Palm Springs Walk of Stars". This was a good place to meet friends, celebrities, and lots of other great people… and get my picture taken for publicity. There they "wrote peoples names, and about their works, on the sidewalk so folks could remember them". Sounded like a good idea to me.

Kaye and Debbie…

***What a Hugg!!… I'm** "Seeing Stars"… again!*

Dad said he had met her years ago, so when the fabulous Debbie Reynolds got her "Star", we were there. People seemed to love Debbie, and wrote her name on the sidewalk… to prove it. She was very pretty, and she said I was too. She and Kaye Ballard (who held me for a long time… as I probably reminded her of **Miss Emily and Sally**… her two "fur kids") hugged me "real tight" and they wanted their picture made with me. You can bet Dad had his camera ready then. I overheard them and pretty Ruta Lee talking about something called "The Thalians"… Dad said it was a group of thespians (actors) that were doing good work for lots of young humans…who had some problems. That made Dad and me feel real good. After all, I am a pretty good *"thespian"*…and I also loved helping people.

"Ruta Lee and Mee"…

Debbie's Star... *"A girl can dream"*   *"Please Mr. Mayor...my hat "*

That day, the Mayor Kleindienst, and many more of our friends were there. I also met and was hugged by other "famous" people, including Alexandra and Sidney Sheldon, and Jim and Jackie Lee Houston... who also held me and hugged me good.

When Ruth Gibson received her "STAR", we were there. She was a sweet lady...and funny. I liked her and she liked me, and Dad too. Dad was right... there were many nice and important people at these events. That day was great and I also had my picture made with Ruth, Herb Jeffries and Richard Harrison.

Ruth Gibson...gets her "STAR(s)"   After the party... Ruth, Herb, Richard

(She said I should get one too)   (Ruth is holding our card)

Kirk Douglas... *"Unforgettable"*   *"He petted me so tenderly"*

 Dad had seen him in western and action movies, and said he played "tough". Then one day in downtown Palm Springs, at one of his book signings...we met Kirk Douglas. Dad said he was famous and would remind me the next time we saw him on TV. Even though Dad said he had recently had a stroke, he looked fine to me. While we were having our picture made together, he took time to ask about me, and gave me a real soft and gentle caress. I felt his tenderness...his kindness...like a Grandfather. I liked him. Dad sent him prints of the pictures, and he sent us a letter thanking us. See... I felt it...*WE just know these things*. He was really nice

"Sparkling" (*like me*) Joey English, whom we knew, also got a "STAR" on Palm Canyon. We liked it when she rode up on the back of a big Harley...*ironically with a preacher.* (Dad, as he had taught so many women to ride, would have liked it better had she been riding it *solo*). Anyway, we were invited to her "Joey English Radio Show". On the show, she was talented, talked pretty, and did it well. I didn't say much, but Dad talked, so "everyone knew I was there". Joey loved me, and even said so ...*on the Radio!!!.*

Joey..."Radio & TV"...and Mee

We had heard her on the Radio, and seen her pictures, and wanted to meet her.

So, meeting for lunch at Sherman's Deli and Bakery (yummm), we met Kate Porter... a

special human that really loved animals. (28 'babies' at last count) She rescued them, wrote about them, and had a radio program dedicated to them. In the past, Dad also had a television Show, so they got together with an idea for a television program "about animals and their families". They talked about me being on with them while they did a 'man and woman talk show'. We even went to the TV station and talked to the Program Director, and also to Ann, a nice lady who was a Vice President of what they called V.P. of Marketing. She was nice, and told me I was too. I was thinking… *"Me on TV... a Star... this is what I was born to do"*... However, for some reason the plan didn't work out and Dad felt sad. So for a while I had to give him some…

Kate... *did love me too, (Also)*   …special attention. Later however, Kate got one going and "Animal Chat" began on local cable television. Kate did come to our house, and Dad and I did one of her first '*in home interviews*' for the Show. Wow… I was on TV, and maybe now we could do some more good for everyone. Dad was feeling *a little* better now.

During this time, through Donna, I was getting some offers for modeling gigs. I kept her busy keeping me "beautifully groomed". I did several modeling jobs, some for major companies, and some for local businesses', which Kate filmed and edited for us. Dad says… *"Three things sell…a cute pet, a pretty woman, and a pretty car."* Case in point…*here we've certainly got two of those covered and this should certainly entice anyone to buy… almost anything.*

"Models…striking a pose"

From: Valerie-Jean-Hume   (Email...)
To: <Gracie@desertdailyguide.com>
Sent: Thursday, February 17, 2000 5:33 PM
Subject: Thank You

Dearest Gracie.

What a photogenic puppy you are! Please thank your Daddy for sending me the photos of the two of us. You certainly are gorgeous, not to mention a terrific journalist! Who would have guessed?

Thanks again!

Love love vj   *VJ and Me..."A happy hugg..."*

Among all these public appearances... I enjoyed the parades...the big Christmas Parade... The Veterans Day Parade... and the Gay Pride Parade. (We weren't 'gay', but we were 'happy', and were invited, and enjoyed ever second of it)

Then through Robann's Jewelers, and Diane Mori who worked there, and who told Josh and Benjamin of Uneek Jewelers in L.A. about me... "Because of all the good deeds I was doing" donated to me, a very expensive gold collar. **So then...** *" Adorned with my new gold collar, inlaid with fifty, 25 carat, princess-cut-stones", And with Dad pulling me in my little red wagon... with "P.A.W.S" written on the front and back... and with "Driving Miss Gracie" written down each side"...while sitting on, a gold-fringed white silk pillow... ringed with a red and white boa... under a white silk Brocade umbrella"...then*

*"A Happy Camper".   ...occasionally getting out of my "ride" to work the crowd... **we worked the Parade** "*

(That scene...got my picture and the story...in the Desert Sun.)

Every girl needs a little "bling"...

Diane..."Thanks for the necklace"

"Driving Miss Gracie"...check the ride

"I love my ride" ...... but I could get used to "this"...for our other car.

Bill and Jerry ...
"A refrigerator picture"

Adjoining Spencer's Restaurant, at the Palm Springs Tennis Club, Dad and I attended the Bill Edelen Symposium every Sunday morning, and where I was... according to Bill, "a charter member." Dad liked him and so did I. Other "Pets" were welcome there. Attendants of the Symposium were very special people and many became our close friends. Bill and wife/Jerry introduced us to Tai and Chi., their two Shitzus... "The real heads"... of the Edelen household.

"From The Edelen Symposium, and also a big contributor to Animal Samaritans, we met a nice lady named Suzi Ficker. Suzi sang with an operatic voice, and for years was also "an avid racer, and Championship Cup Holder", of big world-class sailboats." Susie loved me, and introduced me to her two 'children'…Baby (a small 'mix'), and Eesa (a large Coyote-Shepard mix). Susie once made the statement that I was *"a binding link between animals and humans"*, and *"with the ability to bring both together, and with each other…and that I should never be forgotten".* That was pretty profound. Dad thought so too… and *got a little teary-eyed.*

Dad and I were invited to "house sit" for several of our friends and of course they all had "babies", and we loved it. Elaine Murphy, *whom we both really loved,* …lived with her best friends; her three "babies"…**Murphy** (toy poodle), **Matilda** and **Cleo** (handsome 'mutts' both rescued off the streets in Mexico). Elaine was born and educated in Dublin, Ireland. She became a famous model. Then she studied art, and with her natural talent, became a very good artist. She painted one of me, and a life-sized portrait of Dad and me, and presented it to us at the Bill Edelen Symposium. Even after Elaine moved to Laguna Niguel for a while, we went there to see her and her "babies". Sometimes we stayed a month or two. I loved it. About this time I was beginning to feel "under the weather"… however *"This beautiful and affluent environment… seemed to make us all feel better."*

Brenda Berman was a sweet lady… We met…became good friends…and stayed over to 'sit' with her "babies". All are Maltese. **Brutus** (the boy), **Pearl** and **Lacy** (the girls). She loved them all, but Lacey was a favorite. Brenda loved me too… and we *all* got along real well.

Pearl   Lacey   Brutus.

Brenda and Lacey…

Colby, (my sweet) Lindi, and "*Moi*"

Lindi Biggi, with whom Dad and I had helped get closer acquainted with Animal Samaritans, (and the rest is history) was always so gracious to us on our visits to her beautiful home and gorgeous estate grounds. What a great place to play and show off my "running" skills. And, with her many tropical birds, and five precious "children"… **Luigi Biggi, Squeegie Biggi, Feigi Biggi, BG Biggi and Gigi Biggi**…What a crew…(**"BG"** and **"Gigi"** ' are even smaller than me). We all talked and giggled at their "cute" names, and also how sweet and how much fun their Mom was. "We love our Mom and feel so fortunate to have her, and to be here". They also said, "anything Mom calls us (*especially for lunch*) is fine because we know how much she loves us". I certainly knew that feeling… and *we all got a little 'misty eyed'.* We all played together and it was great fun to be with others my size … and even smaller. Then seeing Gino (her husband, whom I only met once) joining them, we all ran back to be with them and wait for a healthy treat. …*Yep, we got one.*

Speaking of Lindi's generosity… because I was getting weaker physically, she and Dad had discussed having the soon celebration of my next birthday at her home. Wanting to combine this with a fundraiser for Animal Samaritans, and to invite "some well-known celebrity"…a cute little pooch named **"Mr. Winkle,** had become quite famous on TV, and on the Internet…(Over a million hits). So Dad and I went to Los Angeles to meet him

Laura Jo and "Mister Winkle"…*at my birthday party…I love the green*

and his pretty Mom… Lara Jo Regan. Lara Jo is an award-winning photographer, known for her interpretive documentaries, and has a background in Anthropology. (Also while there, we met a film crew from Japan who were shooting a 'special' of Winkle, and they asked if they could come to Palm Springs and shoot one of me. Dad said yes…they did… and I went "International".) We invited Mr. Winkle and his mom to my birthday party to be given at Lindi's beautiful home and estate. Lara Jo came and brought some of Mr. Winkle's "famous calendars. We all had a ball…raised some money for charity… and took plenty of pictures to remember.

Me and "Winkie" …*Posing for Charity.*

Sometimes things got a little (very) rough financially for Dad and me. At Bill Edelen's Symposium, Gayle Hodges, a very sweet lady heard about it. She was a lover of animals and people… and loved me lots. She and her husband Chuck 'came to our rescue' and also later helped us in many other ways. We were just among the many they had helped. (They are most gracious to Charities and Causes in the Valley, both animal and human.) At this time I was not feeling so good health wise, and Dad was really worried. Their help made things much easier, especially at this time.

Chuck and Gayle…*loved me too*

Madelyn Hinsvark also heard, and again "kept us from being (literally) on the street". She is a beautiful lady, an animal lover, a real strong contributor to Animal Samaritans and the "Mom" of her beloved (Lab Mix) Bonnie. Madelyn, and her husband Ken, also loved us… and loved what we were doing for some of our less fortunate "brothers and sisters".

Madelyn and Me…*"A love hugg"*

Dad, who for most of his life had given so much to others, understood the discomfort of "having to ask for help"... But he was not too proud to ask ...or to receive it...considering what the results might have been... if he had not.

Another family, for whom we would housesit, was our friends **Claude Smithern** and his wife **Paula**. Their two "boys" were **Pierre** (a bichon frise)" and **Tiger** (an Australian Silky). As you can see...this handsome 'French and Aussie combo' liked to be a "little frisky", but I knew how to put the boys in their place, and besides, Dad was always watching... well... most of the time.

Pierre and Tiger...my "Welcoming Committee"

I'm doing lots of things, and meeting lots of people, and visiting people in the hospitals and Retirement Homes... Somewhere along the way, with all those visits, and meeting people, I guess I "contacted something" that weakened my immune system. A new article was due at the Desert Daily Guide, so I wrote about it...

(This was one of Gracie's last articles)

Hello Sweethearts,

   Well, I guess you have heard – My health as blown a few fuses, affecting my heart, my liver, my kidneys, my pancreas and my adrenal glands. The main diagnosis, a human disease called "Cushing's disease". It's not too familiar to everyone, but getting more common everyday...Leave it to me to get a mystery disease. I always do everything with flair. Seriously, I had a very hard time for two or three weeks, and thought I was going to "lose" Dad.

   I won't go into detail, but this is serious enough that I have to take it very easy in order to recover. My daily insulin shot and the hydration (fluid) injection... leaves me not too perky. With these injections, along with medicine for my heart and for the Cushing's disease, I seem to be holding my own and even show signs of slow, but gradual progress for the better.

   I certainly don't want to let any of you down, and I think about your needs, but now I need your help, your prayers and positive thoughts. These can help so much in turning this around. I'm even more worried about "Dad"... he's really hurting.

   I have to take some time off and that makes me sad, but I believe in you, and know you understand. Have faith Sweethearts, there is love in this world... and it's coming your way. Bye Bye

                    Recuperatingly, Yours   I Love You ... Gracie   xoxoxo

"I have met so many great humans, and their "precious, furry, four-legged children" (my brothers and sisters), ... and I would love to mention them all here, and maybe somewhere within this you will see your name, or picture, but even if you don't, please know that I love you, and I know that you loved me. Lately I am getting kinda tired, so I have asked Dad to take over, and with a few pictures, finish telling my story"... Gracie.

A Summary

Gracie...was *"an experience"*. She had a magical, mystical, and unforgettable effect on everyone who saw her, and for those whom were privileged to experience her charms, caused many to comment... "Just too cute", "Extraordinary personality" "She's more like a little Angel". When she went walking on Palm Canyon Drive in Palm Springs, on El Paseo in Palm Desert, or on Rodeo Drive in Beverly Hills, her perky and sophisticated "air" turned every head. Her face and 'figure'...charmed pedestrians, drew crowds, and could stop traffic. She was so perfect many could not believe their eyes. It is true though she had a reputation…as a "lover". She kissed…was kissed …sat on the laps of…and was hugged by…more famed celebrities than most folk will ever meet. She charmed…Movie Stars, Rock Stars, Moguls and Mayors…Singers and Politicians…and literally everyone who saw her.

She was invited to many Coachella Valley special events. Some were given in her honor. She loved to attend the "Palm Springs Walk of Stars" ceremonies. She especially loved the Parades: The Christmas, The Gay Pride, and The Veterans… and who can forget her...in that little red wagon with "Driving Miss Gracie" on the side.

From one admirer, "For Her Many Good Deeds", she was given a beautiful necklace…"with fifty princess-cut, twenty-five carat semi-precious-stones, set in 14 ct. gold". She wore it proudly, with charm and beauty and her unique brand of cute sophistication… to the delight of a few, or to the admiration and applause of many. She did several modeling shoots for big, and some local companies. Because of her many public appearances and as a celebrity and model, she did weekly visits to her special salon for a 'hair and nails' makeover.

Considering her personality and charm, her size was the only thing "small" about her. She was much more than just good looks, she was also a "Dealer in Smiles". Her time was dedicated to helping others. She gave of herself to 'Charities, Hospitals, Nursing Homes, and shut-ins, and many public functions.

A "T.V. Star" on Kate Porters "Animal Chat", she appeared hundreds of times on Television, made appearances on "The Joey English Radio Show", and "made" the Desert Sun newspaper for many of her charitable activities.

In addition to receiving an award from Animal Samaritans…"In Recognition For Her Many Years of Service to the Entire Community", she was also named "Roving Reporter" for their publication "Animal Tales". She was truly their Mascot. She was "a dues paying, special member" of The Palm Springs Chamber of Commerce.

For the Desert Daily Guide, she wrote a weekly news column called "Ask Gracie". Many out of town visitors considered her their "Palm Springs Mascot".

Gracie received a very special award…the "First Annual, Pets on Parade, Canine Ambassador Award" -- To "GRACIE" STEWARD.

She received *"Certificate of Special Congressional Recognition"*…from… Congresswoman Mary Bono.

<><><>

When Gracie was seven years old, she was diagnosed with Cushings Disease, that developed into Diabetes and was given perhaps a month to live. After losing weight and some of her hair, and becoming partially blind… she eventually rallied… to love, medical treatment by Doctor Melinda "Mindy" Byers, special diet formulated by U.C. Davis, and to my personal holistic nutritional supplements. The City of Palm Springs, and others throughout the Coachella Valley rallied to her aid. With the idea started by Marianne Hunnzinger and her daughter Ines, the Downtown Merchants of Palm Springs displayed Gracie's picture on small collection boxes to help defray the cost of her medical bills. Even small children gave, sometimes a few pennies, others much more…but… gave they did. Through our friend Mike Russell of Animal Samaritans of Palms Springs, and many of its gracious supporters, gendered great support for Gracie. It took a while, but she got her hair back and her energy level was almost normal. She looked great but her eyesight limited her, however she learned to adjust. It made me so sad, but I never saw her complain or register pain. Regularly receiving her insulin shot once a day, Gracie lived another full year and three months. She had such a will to live and I determined that she enjoy every minute of it. I was torn between denial, and the tearful inevitability of what must happen someday. Though extra sensitive to the situation, I determined to be positive, yet not be one who selfishly makes their pet (loved one) suffer, when they get too sick to have a quality of life. To me... *That is cruelty, masked as caring.* So we extracted every ounce of happiness from every moment of every day of our togetherness. I always received her unconditional love.. She never ceased to thrill me and I became more thankful everyday to wake up to her presence. I felt blessed to share her magic with others, and I am a blessed man for the pleasure of over eight years of our love and togetherness. There will never be another Gracie…but if another *Angelic Entity* comes to me… I'll know who sent it… and who approved it.

Last Days Scenes

Marianne and Ines…*comfort me.*   Kim Anderson… *played her Flute…to help me heal.*

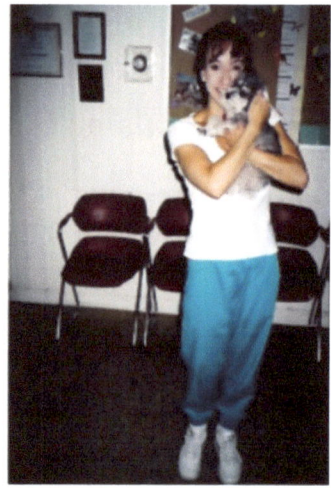
Ronda *gave me shots...with love.*
(Desert Animal Hospital)

Kate... *giving me comfort ...*
(Loma Linda Hospital)

(Desert Sun) ... Gay Pride Parade (last)

"When the Tiara tilts...its time to go"

"My favorite place to be...at the end of a perfect day"

I've been feeling a little tired these days ... just need a little rest...So until the morning ... Good night Dad ... I Love you...

Finally succumbing to pancreatitis, Gracie mercifully, slipped into a coma. Even then, only after carrying her warm, precious, barely breathing little body through the house, from room to room in my arms, and convincing her that it was 'all right to', could she…or I…give up to let her go. The next morning after several phone calls and gathering at the Desert Animal Hospital, … Marianne Hunnzinger, Kate Porter, Elaine Murphy, Dr. Melinda Byers and many of the staff witnessing, (and with not a dry eye in the room) *Gracie… resting in my hands… peacefully "passed over" to another dimension, and quite conceivably, to new adventures.*

Her ashes are now preserved, along with her many memorials. After Gracie's passing, but with her influence continuing to aid the charity, at their next Holiday Luncheon at The Ritz-Carlton Hotel in Rancho Mirage with near 300 in attendance, Animal Samaritans honored her memory. Kate showed a new 7-minute video she had made of her, and then Kate and I told Gracie's story of "The little dog that everybody loved". In The Desert Sun, along with two pictures of her, she received a five-column obituary entitled "Fans Mourn Passing of Precious Poodle". The Desert Daily Guide wrote a memorial page to her. Congresswoman Mary Bono sent a personal letter of condolence from her Office. Dozens of cards and phone calls were received. (Unfortunately, but perhaps because of all the publicity about it, thieves broke into my home and stole Gracie's beautiful collar from her memorial display …*greed truly has no conscience.)* Gracie had lived only eight years and three months. Even though this was relatively a short life span for her breed, she had certainly "lived several lives" and all of them, lived to their fullest. I am so thankful to the Universe (who sent her), and Andrea (who brought her). And for every day we spent together, as my companion, my best friend and the joy my life. Our friends constantly remind me of her, and also when visiting places we often went. For all the love she stirred in me, and also in the lives of others…Gracie will live forever in our hearts.

David Steward… "Gracie's Dad

Gracie

2-3-94   -   5-2-02

Remembered always…with love
a smile…and a tear

"We cannot rest… until the last cage is empty, the abandoned are rescued, the hated are loved, the hungry are fed, and humanity made to feel its responsibility to make it happen…for animal and human alike…then and only then can our joy be full, and the resting from our labors…be truly fulfilled".   …***Gracie***

GRACIE'S WORLD
2-3-94 - 5-2-02